ESCAPE
from
SAIGON

ESCAPE
from
SAIGON

How the church survived the final days of the Vietnam War

Ralph S. Watts

Pacific Press® Publishing Association
Nampa, Idaho
Oshawa, Ontario, Canada
www.pacificpress.com

Designed by Dennis Ferree
Cover Photo: Bettmann/CORBIS

Photos not specifically credited are courtesy of the author.

Additional copies of this book are available by calling toll-free
1-800-765-6955
or by visiting www.adventistbookcenter.com

ISBN: 0-8163-2113-2

05 06 07 08 09 · 5 4 3 2 1

Dedication

To my dear companion, Pat,
and our four children,
Edie, Marcia, Ralph Steven, and Laurie,
for their understanding, support, encouragement,
and prayers.

Acknowledgments

I wish to express my appreciation to RosAnne Tetz, a freelance writer, and to Russell Holt, editor at Pacific Press® Publishing Association, who so ably assisted in the production of this book, and to Esther Brummett for typing the manuscript.

A portion of the proceeds from the sale of this book is being contributed by the publisher and the author to the Adventist Development and Relief Agency (ADRA) and to the Vietnamese Seventh-day Adventist churches. These funds will help support various projects in Vietnam.

Contents

Air Tragedy

More often than I would like, I am asked to tell the story of my experience in the evacuation of a number of Saigon Adventist Hospital employees and church leaders from Vietnam during the fall of Saigon. Whenever I agree to tell this story, I always feel compelled to wear a particular outfit. It's called a safari suit. My wife and I always have a little debate as to whether I should wear it. I always end up saying, "I don't understand why it is that every time you wash this thing, it shrinks." She just laughs at me, because safari suits do not shrink.

I wore this outfit in Southeast Asia, where we lived, because the weather is hot and muggy. As I and other workers traveled throughout the territory for appointments, we felt comfortable wearing something light. This safari suit is lightweight. It washes quickly. And this particular suit of clothes has tremendous sentimental value to me.

I say I am asked to tell this story "more often than I would like" because it was a very traumatic experience for me. When I relate this experience, I relive it. On the night before I must tell the story, I will wake up early in the morning, rehearsing the story, going through the material in detail to refresh my memory. I often lie awake for several hours, unable to go back to sleep, reliving the most event-filled week of my entire life.

What I share with you now is being shared through the eyes of one person—myself. Others who were involved in this episode will have a different version, because they looked at it through different eyes, from a different perspective. What I will share with you will be the experiences, the feelings that I have lived with and will continue to live with for the rest of my life.

At the outset I want to say something very, very important. I am fully aware of the fact that human endeavor did not make it possible for many of our Vietnamese leaders and employees to escape from Saigon. There is no question in my mind that through it all the hand of God was evident. Doors that seemed to be closed were opened through His intervention. I want to give credit today to our God. I want to give glory to His name. That He used us as human instruments in this is beside the point. The important lesson for us is that, uncertain as the future may seem, we serve a God with whom all things are possible. I hope that as this story unfolds you will gain that same understanding.

I want to begin on Friday, April 4, 1975, a few weeks before the collapse of the South Vietnamese government and the fall of Saigon. A very important event transpired on that day that plays a significant role in this whole story.

Two days earlier President Ford had ordered the evacuation of Vietnamese orphans. Perhaps you recall the orphan flights. They received quite a bit of publicity. President Ford had indicated that about two thousand orphans, most of whom were fathered by American servicemen, were to receive high priority in the evacuation, and so through various agencies the children were airlifted out, with adults going along to care for them. Some of our own hospital staff and missionaries were involved in these orphan flights. The flights began on Wednesday, and by Friday they were really going into high gear.

At about four-fifteen on Friday afternoon one of the world's largest aircraft, the C-5A Galaxy Transport, lifted off from the Tan Son Nhut airbase. This aircraft is so large that three jeeps can enter into its fuselage side by side. The two huge cargo doors open up like a clamshell, and these vehicles can drive in. It is a two-decked airplane. On this particular day, a little over three hundred people were on board the plane. The exact count is not known even to this day. As the plane lumbered off with its precious cargo, little did anyone realize, either on the ground or in the air, what was to transpire in a matter of minutes.

The plane ascended in a very tight circle to avoid enemy anti-aircraft fire and then proceeded on an easterly course. It had reached an elevation of about 23,000 feet, over the Gulf of Tonkin. Twenty to thirty minutes following takeoff, it was struck by a terrible explosion. The two cargo doors at the back of the aircraft blew open. Because the plane was at 23,000 feet, decompression obviously occurred immediately. Some of those seated at the very back of the airplane—we don't know how many—were sucked out and fell to their deaths below. These were little children—many of them just babes in arms, most of them under twelve years old. Just kids—packed into that aircraft, some on the upper level, some on the lower level.

When the doors burst open, for some reason the explosion affected the control of the plane's tail assembly, causing the plane to be buffeted about. The only way the pilot could keep the plane flying properly was to ease back on the throttle, but as any good pilot knows, pulling back on the throttle reduces air speed and the plane immediately begins to lose altitude. The pilot made a sweeping circle, hoping to get back to the airbase, but he was losing altitude rapidly.

He was lined up with the Tan Son Nhut airport runways. Just a few miles and they would be safe for touchdown and landing. But the plane, as he reported later, was buffeting terribly. To maintain control he had to keep pulling back on the throttle, and as a result, the plane kept losing altitude. Less than two miles from the runway, the plane lost too much air speed to fly, and it crashed to the ground. It skidded along, jumped over a little stream, plowed on for several hundred yards, broke into several sections, and then burst into flames.

Helicopters rushed to the site and began picking up crash victims who were still alive and rushing them to the nearest hospital for emergency care. Those who were obviously dead were left to be picked up and brought to the hospital at a later time.

The area where the crash took place was a rice paddy that was inaccessible by road. Trucks and ambulances could not enter the area. To make matters worse, just the night before there had been some skirmishes with the Viet Cong right in that vicinity, so the area was unsecured as well. All through the hours of Friday night, U.S. and Vietnamese military and government officials were flying in, trying to save as many lives as possible, and bringing the survivors by chopper to the closest medical facility. The doctors, nurses, and other medical staff at the hospital worked around the clock to save the lives of these little ones who had been so adversely affected by the war. Very few children cried or complained. They were very stoical, very brave boys and girls. Many were airlifted to other places, and treatment was given to those who were able to stay at that particular hospital.

Preliminary reports indicated that 178 were killed outright, and later reports suggested that the number exceeded 200. Probably some 220 or 230 boys and girls lost their lives in that accident. At the time, this terrible tragedy had more casualties than any other airplane accident in American history. Almost without exception, passengers who were in the lower level of the aircraft were killed. When the airplane crashed, it just pushed together like a can that was stepped on. Only those fortunate enough to be on the upper level survived. Seventy to a hundred children survived, and, after adequate medical care, most of these eventually came to the United States.

The reason I tell you this story is because the hospital to which these accident victims were taken was the hospital closest to the scene of tragedy—Saigon Adventist Hospital, operated by the Seventh-day Adventist Church. The hospital was located less than a mile from the airport, and, as I mentioned earlier, the accident took place just a couple of miles on the other side of the runway.

I had left Saigon on the Thursday before this terrible accident took place to return to my home and office in Singapore. The headquarters for the Southeast Asia Union and the Far Eastern Division are both located in the Republic of Singapore, which is about an hour and forty minutes by jet from Saigon. I spent a great deal of time during the early part of 1975 in both Vietnam and Cambodia, trying to salvage what was left of our work.

When my office received the news of the airlift tragedy, we realized that something had to be done to augment the staff of the hospital, yet at the same time we recognized that the situation in the country was quickly falling apart. On Sabbath we received a telex from our leaders in Vietnam indicating that the military and political situation was deteriorating very rapidly. There were questions as to how long we should even continue to operate the medical facility, and they asked for the leadership from the division and the union to return.

And so on Sunday, April 6, I boarded a commercial flight that took me into Saigon. I took a window seat on the right side because I wanted to see what the crash site looked like. As we made our final descent, just before we came over the edge of the runway, I looked out, and I could not believe what I saw. The charred remains of the giant aircraft—the engines, a part of the tail assembly, a part of the fuselage—were scattered over a large area. For those brief seconds that I had to look down as we flew over, I wondered how anyone could have survived that disaster. I went to the hospital to meet with our hospital leaders and talk to them about the future plans, not only for the hospital but for our mission work as well.

The next morning an interesting letter arrived, addressed to Harvey Rudisaile, the administrator, or, as we would say today, the president, of Saigon Adventist Hospital. This letter played an important role as the story unfolded. It was dated April 7, 1975, and here is what it said:

Dear Mr. Rudisaile:

I find it quite difficult to adequately express my personal gratitude and that of my people for the superb medical attention given the surviving victims of the recent air tragedy that deprived us of so many of our friends and the children they were trying to help.

But for the professionalism, devotion, and determination of your staff, that tragedy might well have been total in its consequence.

Please accept our undying thanks and our continued good wishes for your continued help to this community.

Gratefully,

H. D. Smith
Major General, USA
Defense Attaché

"That's a nice letter," we said. "A letter of appreciation from the U.S. government." Mr. Rudisaile posted it on the bulletin board, and we thought little more of it. But in just a short time you will find how significant this letter was. I believe that out of the tragedy that took place the previous Friday afternoon, as sad and heart-wrenching as it was, came a direct blessing to God's people, and to many of our employees in Vietnam at that time.

Saigon: The Last Hope

I need to tell you a little bit about the hospital at this point. Not quite three years before, the United States government had requested the Seventh-day Adventist Church to take over the operation of the large military hospital it had been operating in Vietnam during the war. It was called the U.S. Army 3rd Field Hospital. Readers who served in the military in Vietnam know about that hospital. It was well-known and was probably the best-equipped hospital in all of Vietnam.

We had agreed as a church to provide quality health care, not only for Americans who lived in the country, and not only for the United States government personnel, embassy, and military officials, but also for the Vietnamese. After all, we were not in Vietnam to operate a medical facility just for Americans. Our church's primary mission was to the Vietnamese people, and we did what I believe was a very fine job through the efforts of a wonderful medical staff.

It is understandable that missionaries, physicians, and others would be reluctant to bring their families into this unstable situation. We had only a few physicians there on a regular basis. When we signed the contract to operate this hospital, Loma Linda University Medical Center agreed to help staff the facility. In a cooperative effort with the General Conference, the Far Eastern Division, and the hospital, we were able to bring in physicians on a relief basis, including the heart team, which made several trips to Vietnam. The first open-heart surgery in all of Vietnam took place at the Saigon Adventist Hospital. So the hospital was well-known throughout the country, in the north as well as in the south.

At the same time we recognized that if we allowed a large contingent of Americans to reside in the country under these deteriorating circumstances, at some point we could be caught in a very awkward situation. Early in April 1975 we decided that we must phase down the level of personnel, particularly of American personnel. We scaled back to a skeleton crew—just enough to maintain the hospital and to provide the quality of care that was required.

Beginning about April 6, the morale of South Vietnam was at a low ebb. The people had lost confidence in their own government and their military—for good reasons. They had begun to lose confidence in the United States and its commitment to South Vietnam. Because of the pressure that was brought to bear domestically in the United States, our president and congressional leaders decided, wisely or unwisely, that no further military aid would be provided to South Vietnamese forces. And so the South Vietnamese were forced to try to hold back the onrushing tide from the north with very little support, while North Vietnam was being well supplied by the Soviets and other Communist nations.

President Thieu soon realized that he could no longer hold the northern provinces of South Vietnam, so he ordered the withdrawal of his troops from that region. The result was sheer panic. You may recall seeing some of those pictures on television. People were going out into the river in little dinghies, trying to catch a freighter that was heading south. Do you remember the people clambering aboard, causing the ships to list because so many had climbed on? Because they feared the ship would capsize, armed soldiers and others on deck hit the hands of those who were reaching the top rung, forcing them to fall back into the water.

Do you recall seeing on television some of those who tried to climb aboard aircraft just as they were about to leave the airport? I'll never forget the picture of a young man who tried to climb into the wheel nose assembly of a jet prior to takeoff. This plane was leaving from Da Nang, loaded with refugees who were fleeing to the South. As the plane lifted off, its speed and G-forces caused him to lose his grip and he fell 200 feet to his death.

Jeeps, wagons, trucks, buses, and anything else that could be used to transport people were confiscated and filled by thousands who were trying to rush to the South, especially to Saigon. The Vietnamese people believed that if there was one place in the country to find security, that one spot would be Saigon. If any attempt was made by the South to save the country, it would center around Saigon. This is why, between April 7 and 20, tens of thousands of refugees tried to make their way into the city.

From every section of the north, from the west, and even from the south, people poured into Saigon. The government had a colossal problem on its hands. What could they do with another million refugees in a city that was already filled to overflowing? How could they provide for these people? They took a very drastic action. Just before the fall of Saigon, they erected cordons around the city to prevent more refugees from coming in. Only those who had relatives to provide for them and guarantee their support were allowed to enter. This action caused sheer panic and confusion. Many would have been far better off had they remained in their homes in the rural areas. But people who are fighting for survival will grasp at any straw. Saigon was their last hope—or so they believed.

Emergency Return to Vietnam

On Friday, April 18, our union staff office in Singapore was on a weekend retreat. We had gone up the coast of Malaysia for a few days of spiritual and physical renewal. Many of us were exhausted. I was enjoying a good time with my family and our union office staff when I received an urgent message from the Far Eastern Division president, Pastor Paul Eldridge: "Please return to Singapore immediately. I am calling an emergency meeting of the Far Eastern Division Executive Committee Friday night in my office."

We almost never convened an executive committee meeting during Sabbath hours. I knew that something extremely critical must have developed to warrant such a meeting, and I was quite sure that it had to do with the situation in Vietnam. So I said farewell to my family and the office staff, jumped into my car, and headed back to Singapore.

Friday evening at seven-thirty we met in Pastor Eldridge's office. He had gathered together the latest information from various sources—from our national leaders in Vietnam, Harvey Rudisaile, hospital administrator, the United States government, Loma Linda University, and other sources. There was a deep concern and conviction that the time had come to shut down the hospital, get the missionaries and medical personnel out, and evacuate as many of our national leaders as possible. Someone needed to go to Saigon, break the news, start the preparation, and begin implementation. I was elected.

I knew that it was my responsibility. I was chairman of the hospital board and of the publishing house board. I felt a tremendous sense of responsibility for our work in Vietnam, for Harvey Rudisaile, for the doctors and others who were still in Saigon, and for our Vietnamese leaders whose lives I knew were, without question, in jeopardy. We had known for some time that mission president Le Cong Giao's name was on a North Vietnamese "hit" list. There was no question that if he remained behind when the Communists took over, he would be killed. And there were others in that same category.

You may wonder why the lives of our Vietnamese leaders would be in jeopardy. There were several factors. Because of their close relationship with the church, many of these leaders had left the country and attended meetings in Bangkok and Singapore. Some of them carried heavy positions of responsibility. In some of these developing nations there is a perception by the leadership that churches are simply fronts for the CIA. The Communists in Vietnam were convinced that those who worked for the church in key leadership positions were acting on behalf of the United States government. It is not hard to see why they might come to this conclusion. Where, after all, is the capital of the United States located? And where is the headquarters of the Seventh-day Adventist Church located? You may smile at this, but I'm telling you that there are people in the world who believe this. On top of this was the fact that we were operating a hospital under contract for the United States government. Do you see the dilemma? That is why a number of these individuals were marked men and women.

On Sunday morning, April 20, my wife took me to the Singapore airport. I had thrown a few things into my garment bag, and

I had my attaché case. I travel lightly—I don't like to check anything. Pastor Don Roth, the associate secretary of the Far Eastern Division, had been designated to go with me. The two of us were to go in on Sunday and ascertain what the situation was. Others would be coming in on Monday, and then we would make a final determination as to what would happen as far as the work in the hospital was concerned.

As I embraced my wife I said, "Pat, come back to the airport on Wednesday night. I'm scheduled to return on Air Vietnam. I'll be arriving in the afternoon. Be sure and meet me." I had to return to Singapore for several reasons. I had a union mission committee the next day, a hospital board meeting, and a college board meeting. My plan was to go into Vietnam on Sunday, come back on Wednesday, and return to Vietnam the following Sunday. But you know, our good wives sometimes have special insight, and she said, "You'd better be prepared to stay a little longer."

During this time the new reports coming into Singapore were very depressing. Because of a blackout of news, those of us who were in Saigon did not have all the information that was being communicated around the world. You were inundated in the U.S.—on radio, television, and in newspapers. Some of these reports were accurate, and some were not accurate. But even with our limited information, we in Saigon realized that the situation was very serious.

After talking to our hospital and mission leaders, Don and I recognized that we were faced with several major decisions. One of the most urgent was how long to keep the hospital open. Some of the expatriates on the medical staff wanted to close it immediately. They had been pushing this for several days. Others on the medical staff said, "No, not yet. Let's keep this hospital open just as long as we can because we are valuable to this country. They need what we have to offer. Let's not fold up our tents just yet and leave."

I learned through this experience some very valuable lessons. One is that you never can predict how an individual will react to a very difficult situation under stress. Some who I would have thought could handle just about any situation surprised me. They were not able to cope with it. We soon recognized this. We ordered some to leave because their presence was a liability to us. Others, whom we would least have suspected, handled the pressure beautifully. We each have a capacity for a certain level of stress. That's nothing to be ashamed of. It's just the way we are put together.

In early April 1975, we had thirty-six Americans and dependents working at the hospital. On Sunday, April 20, when I flew in with Don Roth, there probably weren't more than eight or ten. One of the first things that we did after our arrival in Saigon was to sit down with Harvey and other leaders and decide which of these would leave the country right away. We developed a system of reducing the number of expatriate medical people. Some were out within twenty-four hours, others within forty-eight hours. Every one of these people had done a good work for us while they were there, but for them to have stayed longer would have made matters more difficult for us. In addition, we felt that in the course of a few days their services really would not be required.

When I arrived at the hospital, Mr. Rudisaile indicated that the American deputy ambassador would be meeting with us. We gathered in Mr. Rudisaile's office with Mr. Lehman, the deputy to Ambassador Graham Martin, along with Dr. Dustin, the chief medical officer for the United States embassy. Dr. Dustin worked very closely with our medical staff and with Mr. Rudisaile to decide what was needed to provide adequate coverage for Americans residing in the country, as well as in meeting the terms of the contract that we had signed with the United States government. They tried to reassure us.

Already there had been indications from our medical staff that we needed to close the hospital and get out as quickly as we could. But there were other factors involved. What about our Vietnamese employees? What about the patients? What about our obligation to the nearly six thousand Americans still residing in the country? What about the U.S. embassy and the embassy personnel from other countries? We couldn't just walk off and leave them. We needed assurance from the deputy ambassador that arrangements would be provided, so that if the situation warranted, our people would be able to leave without the loss of lives. He gave us that assurance—or he tried to.

Some of us felt rather skeptical. We said that we wanted a plan clearly outlined on paper by the embassy or by the United States government for the evacuation of both our U.S. personnel and our key Vietnamese who had worked so faithfully with us in the operation of this facility. We asked him to give us that plan. He said that he could not do it that afternoon. He would review our request and talk with us the next day.

The Beginning of the End

On Monday, April 21, three more persons from the division and the union office arrived: G. O. Bruce, treasure of the Far Eastern Division, Romie Gainer, treasurer of the Southeast Asia Union, and Royce Thompson, who was in charge of our hospitals for Southeast Asia. That same day we divided into teams and began making our contacts. Some went down to the embassy, others called on Dr. Dustin, while others contacted the ambassador's office. One team was appointed to keep up with intelligence reports. The intelligence office in the United States embassy was not called the intelligence agency or the CIA. It was referred to as the Political Office. We worked with three key people: Mr. Lehman, Mr. Currier, and Mr. Bordeaux. We contacted these individuals regularly during the next few days to try to find out exactly what was happening in the country.

Unfortunately, all we got was a lot of double-talk. We were not told the truth. We were told confidentially that there was a tug-of-war—a major policy debate—going on in the United States government between the Pentagon and the Department of State, between Ambassador Martin and Secretary of State Henry Kissinger, and we in Vietnam were caught in the middle. The issue was what to do about Americans and key Vietnamese. Saigon was surrounded by sixteen armored divisions of the Viet Cong. Sixteen divisions! They could have walked in and taken the city at any time, with almost no resistance. The city was like a ripe plum, ready to be plucked. But the United States government was in the midst of a controversy!

Ambassador Graham Martin had a theory. He proposed that an evacuation of Americans, of third-country nationals, and of Vietnamese closely associated with Americans would be a signal to the North Vietnamese that we (the supporters of the South Vietnamese government) were throwing in the towel, and that they could take over the rest of the country. The best strategy, he contended, was for everyone to stay on, because there was no way that the North Vietnamese would attack Saigon with the possibility of the loss of American lives, causing the United States to reenter the war in reprisal for the lives of Americans. He saw this as the only hope for some kind of agreement, cease-fire, or arrangement with the North, short of total surrender. Does that make sense?

The military advisors, the Pentagon, and the generals argued that inasmuch as the city was completely surrounded, the North Vietnamese had probably already pegged a date when they were going to move in. They were convinced that public opinion in America would not warrant any further involvement on the part of the United States government. The military officials said, "If there is to be an evacuation, let it be orderly. If it can be done in an orderly process, then we can get the people out. But if we have to do it under severe time constraints, under panic, under difficult conditions—if fighting breaks out, if a battle looms, or if there is no security, then we will not be able to get these people out, and there will be a loss of life."

This conflict of strategy was taking place on Monday and Tuesday, April 21 and 22. Little did we realize that Admiral Morrison of the Seventh Fleet had helicoptered in, met with the ambassador, and told him, "You're dead wrong. We've got to start getting these people out of here!" And the ambassador had said, "Until I hear from Washington, D.C., from the President or Secretary Kissinger, we're not moving."

The turning point took place on Monday night, April 21. President Thieu went on television and, after a ninety-minute speech, resigned the presidency of the country. He said, "I no longer feel that I can govern this nation. We have been asked to enter into the ring with the heavyweight championship of the world at stake. We are one fighter; the North is another fighter, but the difference is this: We have chains tied to our wrists, and we are being asked by the West to fight our opponent. We can no longer fight." Immediately an interim government was put into place. President Thieu was finished.

I can't document it, but I believe that the next morning President Ford, in consultation with Henry Kissinger, ordered the ambassador to accelerate the evacuation of personnel, because immediately the evacuation flights began to speed up. Evacuation flights had been taking place all along, of course, but many of the planes were leaving half empty. But on Tuesday morning, April 22, we saw a difference. By the end of the day we could see that the evacuation had accelerated to the point that planes were coming and going every twenty or thirty minutes—C-130s, C-141s, and other large cargo aircraft.

The first people to leave, obviously, were the Americans. Many of these were exmilitary persons who had come back and were working in Vietnam in their own businesses or as contractors. Many of them had Vietnamese wives and families. Then we noticed that third-country nationals were leaving. These had been contracted from other governments. Then we began to see a flood of Vietnamese people making their way to the airport. But there was nothing yet for us—no word, no definitive plan. We were becoming quite concerned!

On Tuesday we began to make some very crucial decisions. We met at the mission office and asked ourselves about the future of the mission. What about our employees? What about our pastors? What about our teachers and other workers? What could we do to provide for them? How would they provide for themselves? We determined several things. If an evacuation were to take place, some of the key national leaders would have to leave. But then what would we do about the future leadership of the church? Who would take over the operation of the church and its institutions after the present leadership left? How would the church take care of itself? We realized that if we made an assignment or appointment—if we should designate the new president, the new secretary, the new treasurer, assistant administrator of the hospital, publishing director, or publishing house manager prior to the fall of the country, the individuals we appointed would be marked men and women. So we decided to do nothing as far as future leadership was concerned. As hard as it was for us, we left it for those who remained behind to organize themselves and select their own leadership.

Then we brought together all the funds we could find to give to the employees of the hospital, the publishing house, the schools, and the mission. During the few days that remained we wanted them to go out and buy rice and other staples, providing for themselves for as long as they could.

That's what we talked about at the mission office. At the hospital we had a decision to make: How long should we keep the hospital open? I don't know how many patients we had in the hospital at that time, but there were quite a few. We knew there was no way that as Seventh-day Adventists we could just turn the lock on the doors and walk off. Our church would never operate that way. We had to initiate an orderly phaseout of the hospital operation. After consulting with government officials, with Dr. Dustin, and with others, we decided to begin closing down our operation of the hospital by the end of the week. Most of our physicians would be gone, and we notified government officials that they should not plan on any further medical coverage from the Saigon Adventist Hospital following the end of the week. They said they wanted a little time to think it over before they responded. But that was the course we set.

That same day, on Tuesday, some of the hospital leaders asked if they could meet with me and two or three of the other men from the union and the division. They told us that they were willing to stay by as long as the hospital could stay open, if, somehow, arrangements could be made so that in the event of an evacuation, their wives and children could leave. There was no way we could give this assurance, because we had no indication at that point that any of our people would be able to leave.

However, later that day the Medivac flights began. Soon we were able to get some of our nurses, paramedics, and technicians out to the airport, and they were able to leave the country on some of these Medivac flights, making their way to the Philippines, and eventually to Guam. This process began for us in earnest on Tuesday, April 22, and many of these individuals were beginning to leave. In fact, later on in the week we found that we were faced with a real crisis. We were losing so many key staff that it appeared we might not have enough left to operate the hospital.

Some rather ingenious methods were used to get some of our Vietnamese people out to the airport. Quite a few who boarded these flights had casts on, but no broken arms. Others had casts or splints on their legs, but they did not have injured legs. These apparent injuries got them into an ambulance and through the airport barricades, and some miraculously were able to board those flights that took them out of the country.

Some of our people left with no notice. They boarded the plane with only the clothes they had on their backs at the time. They did not even have an opportunity to say goodbye to their loved ones.

As the opportunities developed, we would tell them, "We have made arrangements for you to leave. If you can go, you will have to get in the ambulance right now. Are you ready?"

What would you do if you had to make that decision? That's the kind of decision many of our Vietnamese people made.

Getting the People Out

On Tuesday night I went down to the American embassy to get in touch with the General Conference of Seventh-day Adventists, our world headquarters. It was virtually impossible to communicate outside of Vietnam by telephone or telex. We couldn't call the division office or the union office, or even telex them with any reasonable guarantee of success. The way to be sure of communicating with the outside world was to go down to the embassy, get on the secure phone in the ambassador's office or his assistant's office, and call the General Conference. We gave them the current status and vital information and asked them to relay it on to the division and union office, which would then reassure our families that we were well and everyone was safe. Pastor Duane Johnson was the officer in the General Conference assigned to work with the Far East. Each night I went to the embassy, called, and gave him a report of what was happening. I told him who had left the country that day and who had remained behind, and asked him to contact the families. On Tuesday night I gave what I thought was my final report, because I was scheduled to leave on Wednesday.

I had been asked to have worship for our Vietnamese staff at the hospital on Wednesday morning. Many of the mission employees were there, including employees from the publishing house and the schools. We had asked them to stay fairly close to the hospital in case word came for authorization for evacuation. That way we could communicate quickly and get them out as soon as possible. My heart was very heavy, because I was leaving in a few hours to go back to Singapore. I felt extremely uneasy about the way things were going. As I looked out into the faces of that group of fifty or sixty that had gathered for worship, I thought, *What do I say at a time like this? What kind of encouragement can I give?* We had no assurance at that point that anyone was going to leave. No guarantees. Just double-talk. *What do I do? What do I say?*

I gave a few words of encouragement and exhortation, and then I recalled a scripture that meant a great deal to me. Obviously, today it means even more. The passage that I read that morning is found in Jeremiah 32:26, 27: "Then came the word of the Lord unto Jeremiah saying, Behold, I am the Lord, the God of all flesh: is there anything too hard for me?" We talked about that. We talked about the closed door. We talked about the fact that even though hundreds and thousands were leaving, and even though we did not know what the future held for any of us, somehow we had to believe that it was in God's hands and that He would do what was best for us. He would not turn His back on us. "Is there anything too hard for me?" Those are God's words. We prayed, were dismissed, and went about our assignments.

I went down to the embassy one more time to get the latest information from the political officers. The situation was getting worse by the hour. I wanted desperately to stay, but I knew I had to return to Singapore. I returned to the hospital to meet one of the division officers, and together we headed out to the airport at ten-thirty. We cleared immigration and customs. I checked my garment bag—one of the few times that I have ever done that—

and boarded the airplane, expecting that in a few hours I would be back home with my wife and family and staff at the headquarters in Singapore.

We sat in that Air Vietnam Boeing 727 in the hot tropical sun for nearly one hour, soaked with perspiration. The plane was packed full because thousands were trying to leave the country. There was no word, no indication of what was happening. Finally the pilot came on the intercom and announced that the plane had experienced some mechanical difficulties and the flight was delayed. Would we please disembark. So we all got off the aircraft.

I went up to the station manager of Air Vietnam. I had flown in and out of there so often that he probably thought I lived in Saigon. Although I did not know his name, he recognized me, and we visited for a few minutes. Fortunately, his English was quite good.

I asked, "About how long do you anticipate it will take for this plane to be fixed?"

He said, "It will probably take two hours at least. Two, maybe three hours."

I had cleared immigration and customs. "If I get back here by two-thirty or three o'clock, will that be adequate?"

"Yes," he said, "but where are you going?"

"I've got to get back to our hospital."

"Well, you're not supposed to. You can't do it."

I said, "I need your help. Is there any way that you can let us out of here so we can go back and take care of some urgent business?"

He looked around and said, "Follow me." We followed him over to a side gate. He opened the gate and let us out.

We grabbed a taxi and made our way to the hospital, which was less than a mile away. It was noon when we arrived. Some of the missionaries were eating and discussing the latest developments. From a report I received at that time from some of the men who had just returned from the embassy, I realized that the situation was even worse than I had thought. Reports now indicated that the country would not last more than a week to ten days. *I'm cutting it pretty close,* I thought. *If I leave today [Wednesday] and return on Sunday, that means that we have three days, maybe seven, after I get back before the country collapses completely.* We talked it over and worked on some plans for a Medivac flight.

By this time Don Roth, who was with us from the division office, had worked out a plan to take a number of employees out, including the wife of our mission president, her family, and some of the other key leaders, their wives, and their dependents. How he was able to pull this off I don't know to this day, but he made some contacts and was able to get authorization to put them on an evacuation flight. When he left the following day, to our surprise, about thirty-six people left with him.

About two-thirty we went back to the airport. There was no way I could go back through customs and immigration again, because they had already marked my passport that I had left. I had to wait until I found that station manager. Soon I found him. I motioned to him, and he came over, looked both ways, opened the gate, and said, "All right, go on in." We went in, sat down, and waited on board the plane.

Then we waited. And we waited. It was midafternoon, and the heat was unbearable as we waited for that plane to take off. About an hour later the pilot came out of the cockpit into the cabin with a microphone and announced that this plane would not be going to Singapore. It was being diverted to Bangkok. Later in the evening, another aircraft coming in from Hong Kong would be taking passengers to Singapore who were scheduled on this flight. And so, for the second time, we disembarked. I wasn't going to sit around the airport. There was work to do, and I needed to get back. So once again I looked for my friend. When I found him, I started to ask, but he didn't even bother to talk about it. He just walked over to the gate.

"What time should we be back?" I said as he opened the gate.

"The plane is scheduled to leave at seven o'clock. You should be here by six-thirty."

So I went back to the hospital and met with Harvey, some of the physicians, and others to get a little update on what was happening. As I listened, I felt ill at ease. A terrible uneasiness swept over me that something was not right.

I had a few moments to go up to my little apartment, so I crossed an alleyway, and as I started up the steps into the little room that I had upstairs, coming down the stairs was a man by the name of Eugene Domke. Gene was our maintenance director. He was in charge of the whole physical plant. And all of a sudden it hit me. Gene was a Canadian, not a U.S. citizen, and the Canadian embassy had closed two days previously. I thought, *How will Domke get out of here? Will the United States government guarantee that he will be taken out?* I didn't know. I wasn't sure. When I saw him, I was impressed to make a decision.

I said, "Gene, how quickly can you be ready to leave?"

"What are you talking about?" he said.

"How soon can you leave the country?"

"Oh, fifteen or twenty minutes."

"Pack your stuff and let's get going. Meet me here at six o'clock."

At six o'clock we pulled the ambulance into the little alleyway. Gene came down with his suitcase. We jumped into the ambulance and made our way out to the airport. The plane was scheduled to leave at seven o'clock. I looked for my friend. This time I had a real problem. I wasn't going to be on that airplane. I finally found him, and he came over. We chatted for a little while off to the side of the building.

I said, "I have a real problem, and I need your help."

"What is it?"

"I'm not taking this flight to Singapore."

He said, "What do you mean? You have everything processed. You've been through customs and immigration. You have your passport, your ticket, everything."

I said, "I can't leave. I must stay here. This gentleman must take my place. Is there any way you can help me out and get him on the flight?"

He looked around. I'm sure he thought someone was watching, because he checked all around, but there didn't seem to be any real problem with security guards. He opened the gate and said, "Come with me."

Eugene Domke made his way out to that airplane, boarded the Air Vietnam Boeing 727, and in thirty minutes he was airborne to Singapore.

My wife, Pat, had been checking with the airline all during the day to find out when my flight was due to arrive because she was supposed to meet me at the airport. She went to the airport to greet me, and there she saw Jerry Bruce, whom she recognized, and another man walking with him that she had never seen before. She wondered what had happened to her husband. Bruce came over and explained what had happened, and she met Domke.

Unfortunately, the closest that she got to meeting me was my garment bag, which was on that airplane. In all the confusion of the day I forgot to get it off the plane. That bag, along with Eugene Domke and Jerry Bruce, made its way to Singapore, and Ralph Watts, with his attaché case and his safari suit, remained behind. I didn't even think about it at the airport. I went back to the hospital, and only then did I realize what had happened. I knew I was in a real mess. Where in Saigon could I find a Vietnamese man who wore the same size clothes as I did? I was stuck with what I had on until relief could be found.

However, I didn't feel too bad, for I realized that God had a reason for this. It hit me that it was important for Domke to leave, and it was important that I stay. I didn't fully sense at that time how important it really was that I stay in Saigon.

On Our Own!

The Vietnamese government had imposed a curfew on Saigon. This meant that from 8:00 P.M. until 7:00 A.M. nobody, but nobody, was allowed out on the street without proper authorization. And so, after 8:00 P.M., the streets were deserted. You would see military vehicles going by, or perhaps some ambulances, but that was it. This was the best time for us to get a lot of work done.

We drove around in a hospital ambulance, because security never stopped them. The American embassy was open at night. Several key people were at work, so we would jump into a hospital ambulance and go down to the embassy. We went out to the airport. We contacted the defense attaché office. We carried on a lot of business between 8:00 P.M. and 1:00 A.M.

Wednesday evening at the embassy I tried to find the chief political officer. He was the intelligence agent who could give us the best information. I finally located him. Just as I was beginning to talk to him, he was whisked away for a high-level meeting upstairs with the "big boys," so his assistant came out, and we chatted for a few minutes.

I said to him, "I have got to know now exactly what the situation is. We're done playing games." I'm going to confess that I was a little angry. I was upset because thousands were now leaving every day. Americans were leaving. There was no problem in getting Americans out, and I knew that. Dependents of Americans, third-country nationals, and many Vietnamese were leaving the country, yet nothing was being done for our employees. The government had promised us weeks before that in the event of an evacuation, our people would be given high priority. Yet nothing was happening.

I said, "I want you to give me the straight story as to what your judgment is. I'm not concerned about what others think. I just want you to tell me how long you think the South Vietnamese government can stand."

He said, "Mr. Watts, four to five days at the most."

"Now, let's quit playing games," I said. "I want you to tell me the facts. Where do we stand on the priority list for the evacuation of our people?"

And do you know what he told me? "I can tell you one thing; you're not at the top of the list."

"Well," I continued, "that confirms what I have believed. Now, what about the commitment that the ambassador and his deputy and the State Department gave to our people? We were assured by Deputy Ambassador Lehman that a plan would be devised. We were told that the hospital would be a staging area and that our people would be given high priority because of their close connection with the United States government and the church."

He said, "I cannot answer that question. That's not for me to decide. I can tell you that others on the list are far ahead of your people."

"Then tell me, how are we going to get these people out?" I asked.

He said, "Mr. Watts, I'll make one suggestion. If I were you at this point, I would not depend on the embassy to work it out for you. You'd better find a way. You'd better find another way."

We had received word earlier that day that one of the men involved in this whole process had been assigned by President Ford to serve as a liaison in the evacuation. His name was Johnson. Little did I realize at that time that this man was personally acquainted with Pastor Giao. He knew Adventists, and he knew the hospital. He knew much about us. Here again you can see how the Lord leads in all of these things. I was told that I had to find him if we were going to arrange for our people to leave. He was the one to contact.

I left the embassy about ten o'clock that Wednesday night, returned to the hospital, and met with our leaders for a few moments. Then I went back to the airbase where so much was taking place.

During the course of the day, from seven in the morning until eight in the evening, it was difficult even to drive into the airbase. People were flocking out of Saigon by the thousands, standing at the entrance to the airbase, hoping that by some sheer miracle they might make their way through the gates and onto a flight. We were told that at times there were five to ten thousand people standing outside the one entrance into the airport! The airport was heavily guarded with military and government officers, and it had big, barbed-wire barricades. The only way to negotiate your way in was to make a very slow, careful S-turn. Everyone who went through there during the day was very closely scrutinized, and unless they had the proper papers or permits, there was no way to get in. And on the inside, hundreds and thousands were lined up, waiting to get on those flights.

The airbase was a huge military complex. Sometimes it was referred to as Pentagon East! You cannot believe how enormous the complex was inside the staging area. It was also heavily guarded by U.S. Marines. As we drove in we could see thousands of Vietnamese waiting for their flights to be called so they could board a plane and be on their way.

But not very many of our key leaders were getting on those flights, and time was getting short. We were faced with an enormous obstacle. I never felt so inadequate in all my life as I did at that time. Oh, how we prayed as we worked during the day. Each of us, in our own way, lifted up our prayers to God. "Please, Lord, show us the way! Open the doors. Help us to know what You want us to do. Give us the wisdom and discernment that we need at this critical time. And above all, help us to keep calm, to be patient, to be understanding."

Some of the missionaries were getting jittery nerves by now, but the morale among our Vietnamese members and workers had reached a terribly low point. They were very discouraged. I'll never forget a meeting I had with some of the young men of the hospital staff whom I had met just the evening before. We had had a rather difficult session. One of the young men stood up, pointed his finger at me, and said, "Pastor Watts, we have lost all of our faith in you and in the church. You're an American. You can go out to that airbase and leave here any time you wish. But what about us? Our lives have been wrapped up with the church and the hospital. We are in jeopardy. Some of us will lose our lives. We were given assurance by the government and the church leadership, including yourself, that every step would be taken to make it possible for those of us who have laid our lives on the line to leave. You have failed us."

That was pretty bitter medicine. I was doing the very best I could under those circumstances, and it was hard to listen to those kinds of accusations. But I could understand their frustration. Had I been in their place I probably would have reacted the same way. That's how tense the situation was. Our people were demoralized. Our leaders were worried sick. They didn't know what the future held for them.

It was Wednesday evening when the chief political officer's assistant at the embassy told me that we would have to find our own way out of the country. As I left the embassy I knew that the man to help us find that way was Mr. Johnson, and I had been told that he would be at the defense attaché's office at the airbase at about ten-thirty. So I quickly made my way over to the airport, and I tried to find Mr. Johnson among the hundreds and thousands of people milling around. The gymnasium had been taken over as a processing center. The bowling alley was now a nursery. Vietnamese mothers with little children packed the twelve-lane bowling alley that had been used as a recreation center until just a few days before. The place was packed with people, and here I was, trying to locate Mr. Johnson.

A short time later I saw a black automobile pull up. Out of the back seat came a man in his early fifties. I looked at him in the dark, and I thought, *Well, this can't be Johnson, looking like this.* He was wearing a short-sleeved, sweat-stained, rumpled shirt. He had two days' growth of beard, his hair was disheveled, and his pants were all wrinkled. I said to myself, *This can't be the man that President Ford has assigned to do this job.* But I went up to him and said, "Are you Mr. Johnson?"

He turned around and said, "Yes."

I said, "My name is Watts, and I must talk to you."

"What is it?"

I said, "Are you acquainted with Saigon Adventist Hospital?"

"Oh, yes. I know the hospital well."

"The United States government promised us that it would make provisions for the evacuation of our key Vietnamese people when the time came," I said. "And Mr. Johnson, we're convinced that the time has come." I recounted my visit with the political officer just thirty or forty minutes previously, and then I said, "Mr. Johnson, we are absolutely at our wit's end. We don't know where to turn. I have been told that you have been given a special assignment to help out with the evacuation process. Can you help us?"

I had talked with our Vietnamese leaders earlier about a basic number that we could agree on in case authorization came, so when he asked how many I felt would be involved in this evacuation, I said, "Probably not more than 175."

"Oh," he said, "we haven't had a group that large go through yet. There's nothing I can do tonight. Why don't you come back to my office in the defense attaché wing at eleven tomorrow morning, and I'll see what I can do. I just can't promise anything at this time."

I said, "Mr, Johnson, all we're asking is that you do what you can for us."

He said, "I'll do what I can."

He left, and we left.

Deciding Who Lives, Who Dies

It was now about eleven o'clock Wednesday night. I went back to the hospital and asked Pastor Giao to call a number of our Vietnamese leaders together. Seven or eight came, and we met in Mr. Rudisaile's office. I turned to Pastor Giao and said, "Pastor Giao, I want to tell you exactly where we are." After I gave him an up-to-date report, I said, "Now I'm going to give you the most difficult assignment that you have ever had."

He said, "What is it?"

"By eight tomorrow morning I want a list of 175 people who should leave the country."

Pastor Giao just shook his head. I'll never forget it. He said, "Pastor Watts, you're asking us to be like God. You're asking us to decide who's going to live and who's going to die."

I said, "That's right. None of us as expatriates should make this decision. We can't do it. It is not our responsibility. That's why I have called you men together. You're the ones who must decide. I want you to weigh it very carefully. In your judgment, decide whose lives would be endangered the most if they were to remain behind. Who should have first priority to leave? I want those names on a list. And furthermore, Pastor Giao, I want you to in-clude in that list the employees of our hospital who are not Adventists. We have just as much of a moral obligation to those not of our faith who are working with us in our institutions as we do to our own people. They stood by us faithfully. You need to keep them under consideration as well. Pastor Giao, I need that list by eight in the morning."

Pastor Giao and his group gathered around the table while I tried to get a few hours of rest. I'm sure there were a lot of tears shed. There was a lot of soul searching, a lot of agony. What family stays? What family goes? They knew that those who were asked to stay might very well lose their lives. How would you like to have to be faced with that kind of a decision? I'm telling you, my heart went out to Pastor Giao and to my Vietnamese brothers who had to make those decisions as they wrestled in prayer that night, asking God to give them wisdom. Throughout the hours of that morning they labored with that decision.

About five o'clock in the morning, when I had been asleep maybe three hours, there was a knock at my door. In a stupor I tried to awaken. I tried to pull on my clothes, and you know the safari suit is all I had. I pulled on my trousers. I don't think I even had the shirt on when I went to the door, and there was a little Vietnamese lady. I recognized her. She was our child evangelism director at the mission office. She burst into tears and grabbed my hand. With tears streaming down her cheeks she looked into my face and said, "Pastor Watts, my children, my children. Won't you please, please help me get my children out so they'll be safe?" At five o'clock in the morning I had no assurance to give her. We had not received any confirmation yet that we could get any of these people out. But she held on, clutching my arm, weeping. And all I could do was say, "Bach, we will do our best. We will do our best. I'm sure that God will find a way." She left and went back to her family, but I couldn't go back to sleep. My heart was heavy. My mind was racing.

At eight o'clock I went to the office, and there were Pastor Giao and several others. Their eyes were bloodshot, and they looked very haggard.

I said, "Pastor Giao, do you have the list for me?"

He handed me a manila file folder. I took the folder, opened it, and began turning the pages. One page, two pages, filled with Vietnamese names. I recognized some of them. Four pages, five, ten, twelve pages. I began to get a little suspicious. Closing the folder, I turned to Pastor Giao and said, "I need to know something. How many names are on this list?"

He didn't want to answer. He said, "Pastor Watts, we did what you asked us to do. You asked us to give you a list of names."

I said, "Pastor Giao, that's not what I'm asking you now. I want to know how many names are on this list." I was beginning to get a little upset.

Pastor Giao dropped his head, and then he looked at me. Tears welled up in his eyes and he said, "Pastor Watts, you'll never know what we experienced during the night. Over and over and over we went as we considered these names."

"Pastor Giao, how many names?"

He said, "Pastor Watts, we did the best we could. We tried to reduce it down to the figure you gave us."

"Pastor Giao, how many names?"

"Pastor Watts, there are 225 names on that list."

I said, "What do you expect of us? We've gone to Johnson. I have asked that possibly 175 be considered. He said that's the largest group that's ever been considered up to this point outside of embassy people. How can we in good faith go back now and tell him that we've changed that from 175 to 225? I don't know what you expect of us. We're doing everything we can." And then Pastor Giao, bless his heart, gave me a little sermon. He said, "Pastor Watts, let me ask you one question. Do you remember the worship that you had yesterday morning? Do you remember that passage of scripture that you read to us? 'Behold, I am the Lord, the God of all flesh. Is there anything too hard for me?' Pastor Watts, all we're asking is please, please try."

Now how would you answer that kind of appeal? I took the file folder, put it in my case, and left.

The General's Letter

Several of us were at Mr. Johnson's office at eleven o'clock that morning. I'll never forget the experience of going down those corridors. Have you ever walked through a large office when it was completely deserted? That's the experience we had. We walked down the long, narrow corridors, and we went to the left, and we went to the right. The corridors were filled with crates. The shredding machines had done their work. The files were empty. This was true at the defense attaché office, down at the USAID office, and even at the embassy, for I'd noticed it the night before. The files were empty, and there was shredded paper all over the place. Most of the offices were empty. The building was virtually deserted, except for a few who were working to the last.

When we arrived at Mr. Johnson's office, we found a note pinned to the door. It said, "Am out of the office. Will not be back until 1:00 P.M." So we left. At one o'clock we came back. About one-thirty Johnson appeared, and he hadn't changed clothes from the time I'd seen him the night before. He looked just as bad. Here was a man who was working around the clock, trying to save lives. I admired and respected him for it. He was putting aside personal comfort and ease for the sake of the people.

He came down the corridor, walked past us, and asked us to follow him. We walked into his office, and he sat down behind his desk. I can picture him now, sitting there. His desk was placed at a catty-corner angle to the rest of the room. He sat down at his desk, leaned back, put his hands behind his head, and tried to stretch and sigh and rest a little bit. Then he said, "All right, do you have your list?"

I handed him the file folder. He took the folder and laid it down on his desk. Then he opened it and began turning the pages. My heart seemed to beat loudly. He turned the pages. He didn't say anything; he just looked at the list, mulling it over. Finally, he closed the folder, looked up, and said, "How many names do you have here?"

I said, "Mr. Johnson, I'm embarrassed, but I have to tell you; early this morning I gave explicit instructions to our Vietnamese leaders that they were not to have any more than 175 names on that list. But when I talked to them several hours later, they shared with me the predicament that they were faced with."

"How many names are on the list?"

I swallowed hard and said, "Sir, there are 225 names on this list."

I'll never forget it. He shook his head, placed the palm of his hand on his forehead, and said, "Gentlemen, I don't know if we can do this. I can tell you one thing. I don't have the authority to authorize this large a group to leave."

I said, "What do you have to do?"

He said, "I've got to go upstairs and talk to the general and his staff. I'll probably have to contact the embassy, and possibly even the State Department and the Pentagon."

I said, "Mr. Johnson, whatever you have to do, please, please, do your best for our Vietnamese people."

He stood up.

"What time do you think we ought to be back?" I asked. "How long will it take?"

He said, "I have no way of knowing. Why don't you come back about three o'clock. I'll go right up and see if I can get an interview and make this case for you." Then he left.

Some of our group went back to the hospital; some of us stayed. We would all have left and come back, but we were worried about what would happen if Mr. Johnson needed further information and no one was there to talk to him. So some of us decided that, much as we didn't want to stay, we ought to. For those of us who stayed behind, that two-hour interval was the longest period of time that we can ever recall, because the lives of so many people were in the hands of so few. We paced those quarters. As close as we were as friends and colleagues, each of us was so immersed in his own thoughts that we hardly even talked to one another. We prayed, pleading with God. We paced back and forth through those empty corridors. You could hear the echo of our footsteps as we walked back and forth, wondering what would be the outcome of our cry for help in this great hour of need for our people.

Three o'clock came. Johnson was nowhere to be seen. Three-fifteen, still Johnson didn't show up. Our anxiety was growing. Finally, at about three-thirty—I'll never forget it, because I looked at my watch—I heard footsteps coming down from the upper floor. And down the steps came Mr. Johnson. I looked into his eyes to see if I could get an answer, but his face was totally expressionless. He walked right by us. And we followed him. He went up to his office, took out a key, opened the door, went inside, and sat down. We followed right behind him and stood right there at his desk. We didn't even sit down.

He took that file folder and handed it back to me, and I just knew that it hadn't worked out. I asked, "Mr. Johnson, what was the decision?"

He handed me a piece of paper. "I have a letter for you. Read it."

And here is that letter:

Embassy of the United States of America
Defense Attaché Office
24 April 1975

To whom it may concern:

The attached manifests are dependents of individuals who have closely associated with the United States government. Because of this close association with us, their lives may be in danger.

H. D. Smith, Jr.
Major General, United States Army

Major General Smith. That was the same general who less than three weeks earlier had sent us a letter of appreciation!

I put the letter in the folder. "Does this say what I think it says?"

"Yes, it does, Mr. Watts. Your request has been approved."

I could have leaned right down and hugged him! You will never in your imagination understand the load that was lifted from my shoulders at that time. We looked at one another and smiled, and we left that office praising God for what had been done.

We found out later that when Mr. Johnson went in to see General Smith, he said, "General, I have a very important request to make of you."

"What is your request?"

"Do you know about the Saigon Adventist Hospital?"

The general said, "Why, of course I know about that hospital."

"General, I believe that we owe those people something for what they have done for us over the years."

And the general said, "I agree. What's your request?"

Johnson explained our need. They contacted the embassy and the United States government. Word came back giving clearance for everyone on that list to leave.

Planning the Exodus

The trip back to the hospital from that office at the airport was a trip that I don't even recall. I was in a daze. But then it hit me. I realized that our work was just beginning. Now we had the responsibility of finding 225 people, gathering them together, and getting them into vehicles. We had the responsibility of getting them out to the airport without a scene and onto their planes.

I rushed to find Pastor Giao. I'm sure he was anxious to find out what had been happening, because he immediately asked me, "Do we have any word yet?"

I said, "We're working on it, Pastor Giao, we're working on it." I had the word, but I couldn't tell him. I knew that if I told Pastor Giao, it would put too much pressure on him. As much as I wanted to tell this man, as much as I wanted to share with him the good news, I could not. His people were hounding him all the time. "What's happening?" "What's the story?" "When are we going to go?" "Do we have any word?" It would have been unfair for Pastor Giao to have to live with that kind of pressure. It was bad enough for me. I didn't want him to have to deal with it too. Furthermore, it was now four in the afternoon and curfew was at eight o'clock. What would have happened had word leaked out immediately that the list had been approved? How many do you think would have been in the hospital at eight o'clock to leave— 225? Or 2,250? I could see that we had the makings of a terrible, terrible, situation, so we decided to say nothing publicly at that point.

I called the missionaries together. We met in Dr. and Mrs. George Weisseman's apartment. At this point, so far as we knew, Jean Weisseman was the only American lady left in Vietnam. She certainly was the only one in our group. I had tried earlier in the week to convince Mrs. Weisseman that she ought to leave, that it wasn't safe for her to stay. I don't know how many of you know Mrs. Weisseman, but you don't change her mind very easily when it's made up. Just ask her husband George. At that time she said to me, "I am not going to leave, except with George. When George goes, I go. You don't have to worry about me. I'll be all right." I got to thinking about it. I'd known her for a few years prior to this. And I realized, *You know, she's right. I won't have to worry about Jean. She'll be just fine.* And she was. She was a great strength to all of us during this time.

The missionaries gathered together. Dr. Bruce Branson and Dr. James Simpson were there. Harvey Rudisaile, Romie Gainer, and Royce Thompson were there. They left their practices, the emergency room, and other places where they were working, and gathered together. There were eight of us. I gave them the report, and I want to tell you, what rejoicing there was. After we visited for a few moments, we fell on our knees on that terrazzo floor, and lifted our hearts in praise to God for opening the door that just a few moments before had been shut tight.

And then we talked about the assignment. I said to them, "There is one appeal I must make to you. You cannot under any circumstances give any indication to any of our Vietnamese brethren of what we have discussed here at this point. They must not know anything about this. At the proper time we will give the announcement, but you must not say anything yet." And I explained why. Then I outlined what we would do to facilitate taking the people from the hospital.

I still have the list of assignments that I gave to our overseas workers that night. It's a yellow worksheet. It says: "Thompson, Branson, and Simpson—stay at the hospital and load the people into the ambulances. Watts, Gainer, and Rudisaile—drive the ambulances from the hospital to the airport. George and Jean Weisseman—go into the airport area and be there to receive the Vietnamese as they get off the ambulances and help them get settled for the night." The list also included assignments for our key Vietnamese leaders: "Giao and Nghiep—contact the people. Le Huu and Do Binh—assist Branson, Simpson, and Thompson in loading the ambulances."

I told them, "Everyone must be at their point of assignment no later than 7:45." Why? Because at 7:45 I was going to give the announcement, and each one had to be ready to fulfill his responsibility.

After that meeting in the Weissemans' apartment, we had an even greater task. We had the authorization for 225 people, and we had the names, but until those names were placed on a manifest authorizing them to get on a specific flight there was no way any of them could leave the country. And so we had to take that list of 225 names back to the airport, back to the gymnasium that was the staging area, and find the proper people who could help us get those names on the manifests.

Romie Gainer and I drove to the airport. When we arrived, I looked at the scene, and my heart sank. I said, "Romie, there's no way we're going to get these names on the list tonight." They gymnasium was filled with people standing in a line. There were three desks, with an American official behind each one. Long lines of people went out of the gymnasium and down the street.

Several hundred were waiting in line to get their names on the list. I thought, *If we stand in that line, we will not be at the desk until Friday midday. What are we going to do?*

We walked down the side of the gymnasium to a side door that was cordoned off with ropes. Standing by the ropes was a big, husky American military policeman. I went up to him, and I said, "You really have quite a job on your hands here, don't you?"

He said, "Yeah, we gotta keep the peace, you know. We had a few skirmishes the last night or two." That was very true. There had been some skirmishes right there inside the compound. But he said, "We're ready. I think we're ready."

I said, "Listen, I've got a problem." I seemed always to be saying that.

He said, "What do you mean?"

I said, "I have an urgent message that I've got to take to the man inside who's in charge. What's his name?"

He said, "It's MacGregor."

I said, "I have an important message from Major General Smith that I've got to get to this gentleman. Is there any way that you could let me through that side door?"

"Yeah," he said. "I don't see any problem. Just crawl under the rope."

So Gainer and I got under the rope, went over to the door, opened it, and headed right for MacGregor's desk—the center one. There were these long lines of people waiting to get their names on the list. Most of them, I'm sure, were eventually able to do that, so I didn't feel too much guilt. Normally, I don't cut in on lines. But this was one time when I felt I had a priority. I went up to MacGregor's desk, and, as soon as he finished with the person he was working with, I said, "I understand that you're in charge of this operation."

He said, "That's right."

I said, "My name is Watts. I have a message for you from General Smith."

He said, "Oh, is that right? What's the message?"

I said, "I have here a list of people that must be put on manifests immediately. Can you help me?"

He said, "Where's your letter? So I handed him the letter, and he read it:

The attached manifests are dependents of individuals who have been closely associated with the United States government. Because of this close association with us, their lives may be in danger.

That memo was the secret key. I said, "We have been told that our group should have a very high priority."

He said, "I don't see any reason why we can't begin processing this. Give me the list."

I handed him the file folder, and I thought he was going to choke. He opened the folder, and he did the same thing that everyone else did. He started paging through it in disbelief.

I said, "Mr. MacGregor, may I make a suggestion?

He said, "What's that?"

"You know, if you work on this by yourself, it's going to take all night."

He said, "You're right."

I said, "Would it be of any help if Mr. Gainer and I sat down beside you at the desk and helped out with it?" I'm always willing to give a little hand when needed.

He said, "I'd appreciate that. Pull up a chair." We pulled up some chairs, sat down beside him, and began to fill out the lists.

"Mr. MacGregor," I said, "there's one thing I've got to ask you. I have made a promise that I need you to help me with."

"What is it?"

"I want these 225 names divided up into eight groups," I said. "The first of our group to leave is led by a lady named Mrs. Jean Weisseman. I want you to make sure that she and her husband will be on the same manifest so they can leave on the same flight, because she made me promise that."

He said, "I don't see any problem with that. These planes are holding anywhere from about 110 to 180 passengers. We should be able to get both groups together."

"Great," I said. "I just want that assurance."

He said, "Let's work on it."

And so we did. We started with Jean's name and added the names of twenty-five of our Vietnamese employees and dependents below hers. We assigned another twenty-five to her husband, another twenty-five to Dr. Simpson, and so on down the list of overseas staff, adding the names of twenty-five Vietnamese to each one. My name was last. I wanted to be the last American Adventist out of the country so that if anything should develop, I would be on hand. I also insisted that our key Vietnamese leaders be on that last flight—Pastor Giao, Mr. Nghiep, Pastor Le Huu, and certain others. I wanted these leaders with me to the very end in case anything unforeseen should develop.

And so the lists were made up. Even with three of us working, it took an hour and a half to prepare those manifests.

The Exodus—and Trouble

We returned to the hospital at seven in the evening. About seven-thirty Dr. and Mrs. Weisseman took their belongings and made their way to the airport. At precisely 7:45 I asked Pastor Giao, Brother Nghiep, and Pastor Le Huu to come into the office. They were, of course, absolutely determined to find out what had happened. They were so anxious to know. It's a joy to be the bearer of good tidings, and this was one time I had that privilege. I turned to the brethren and said, "Gentlemen, we have some good news for you. The request for the entire group of 225 has been approved. We're ready to proceed."

Oh, how joyful they were! They jumped right up out of their chairs.

I said, "Now look, we cannot take the time to rejoice right now because we have much work to do." I turned to Pastor Giao. "You and Brother Nghiep have got to contact those of the 225 that are not presently at the hospital. You have fifteen minutes to get the ambulances to their homes and get them to the hospital. Fifteen minutes. The first ambulance will leave the hospital for the airport at 8:15."

These Vietnamese leaders jumped into gear. They got into the ambulances, went out into the community close by, and began to pick up the people that were on those lists and bring them back to the hospital. We had told them that they were to assemble in the recreation area. Instructions were given to those who were to leave that they could take nothing more than what they could carry in a small handbag. They had to leave everything else behind. All their earthly possessions had to be left behind.

Earlier that afternoon we had asked Harvey Rudisaile and Royce Thompson to clear the hospital area. There were hundreds of people inside the hospital compound. We had security guards there provided by the American embassy. But we knew that there was no way we could get our group of 225 out of the hospital compound as long as hundreds of other people were milling around inside. We had to find a way to clear them out. The guards were able to get most of the people outside of the hospital compound, because most of them were simply people coming to visit the hospital or to see friends.

In addition, we had given instruction to Pastor Giao and to the others who were among the 225 that they were not to bring any of their relatives to the hospital. All the farewells would have to be said, all the tears would have to be shed at home. We could not have families coming to the hospital. It was tough, but you can understand why we had to require this. Only those whose names were on the list were to be there. No family, no friends, no loved ones, nobody but the 225. They were to gather there by 8:00 P.M.

Because the curfew began at eight o'clock and the street would be deserted after that, we had decided not to begin the evacuation process from the hospital to the airport until after that time. There were large crowds of people between the hospital and the airport during the day, and this would have made it impossible for us to carry out our plans, particularly if the crowds had seen what we were doing and realized that people were leaving. So to avoid an unfortunate scene or an incident, we decided to wait until the curfew and take our chances by putting our people in the ambulances. During the darkness of night we would transport them from the hospital to the airport, where Dr. and Mrs. Weisseman would be waiting to meet them.

I want to tell you, my friends, I will never forget the scene as long as I live. I was to drive the first ambulance. I had backed the ambulance up to the recreation area. Inside were Dr. Branson, Dr. Simpson, and Royce Thompson, checking off names with the Vietnamese. As one of our Vietnamese leaders called off the names, the ambulance backed right up against the doors of the recreation building, and those designated were to get into the ambulance. The leaders began calling off names. One of the names that was called was that of the mission treasurer, an older man by the name of Ly Ba Hoi. I heard them call his name, and then a scene took place. I looked inside the recreation building to see Brother and Sister Ly Ba Hoi with their two daughters. Mother and father were on the list to leave, but the two married daughters were not. Their husbands were in the military, and there was no way, obviously, that we could take any military personnel out of the country. That was out of the question. We had promised the government that we would not do that, and we kept our word. These girls obviously could not go off and leave their husbands. At the same time, their mother and dad were leaving, and they believed in their hearts, as they said Goodbye to them, that they would probably never see their mother and father again on this earth. Put yourself in that situation.

We had given instructions that these girls should not be there, but here they were. One daughter was clutching the father, and one daughter was clutching the mother. Their arms were around one another, the tears were flowing, and all of them were crying as if their hearts would break. As I looked at that scene, my heart was aching too. There was a lump the size of my fist in my throat. I thought, *What if I'm ever faced with that? What if I were leaving?*

What if I were having to say goodbye to my daughters? How could they endure it? How much pain can a person take? With all the trauma that they had gone through during the war, now they were leaving their daughters because they knew that if they stayed behind they would probably lose their lives. And yet, how could they turn their backs upon their two daughters that remained behind?

I hated to be tough, but I had to. I went up to Pastor Giao and said, "Pastor Giao, you've got to get those people in the ambulance now." I could see the tears in his eyes as he went over there and put his arm around Brother Ly Ba Hoi, his colleague, and physically helped him and his wife get into that ambulance. We slammed the door shut and left the daughters there, watching as their mother and father rode away. Those are scenes you can never erase from your mind's eye. That experience was repeated over and over during the hours of that night.

A young lady was seated beside me while I drove the ambulance to the airbase, and she was crying her heart out. We came up to the checkpoint manned by heavily armed Vietnamese soldiers. An officer came over—he probably was a colonel—and talked to the young lady in Vietnamese. I found out afterwards that he asked, "Why are you crying?"

"I'm leaving my family and my friends," she wept, "and I'll probably never see them again."

"Young lady," the officer replied, "stop your crying. You ought to be ashamed of yourself. Why are you crying for yourself? You will be leaving this country. Your life is saved. You are secure. You'll go to a new land and make a new beginning for yourself. Young lady, if you cry, you ought to shed tears for those of us who cannot leave, because many of our lives will be taken."

One ambulance after another made the trip. Others had their assignments, so Harvey, Romie Gainer, and I kept the ambulances going. I kept Pastor Giao at the hospital. I wanted to make sure that if we had any problem, I could communicate with him, and he could help me.

We were beginning to make fairly good progress in moving these people from the hospital and out to the airbase. I had just returned from a trip when all of a sudden I could see some agitation. I was standing off to the side while my ambulance was being loaded, and a group of very agitated young people came up to me. They were some of our Chinese young people—Vietnamese, but of Chinese ancestry. They had been born and raised in Vietnam. They knew that as Chinese they could face a very difficult situation when the Viet Cong took over. They came up and said, "Why weren't we notified? Why were we overlooked?" They were very upset.

We had decided and had approval that only employees and their dependents would be eligible to leave through the church's intervention, and I was convinced that these young people were not our employees. I made a brief inquiry, and I found out that some had been, but they were not now. Nevertheless, they pleaded with me, "Please, can't you get us on the list? Can't you see that we leave?"

I said, "There's nothing I can do for you now." Still they kept harassing me, particularly one of the young men. I was trying to go about the evacuation, and he followed me every step, talking, yelling, and demanding.

Finally, I'd had it up to here. I called one of the other young men that I recognized, and I said, "Come here just a minute. I want to talk to you." I had the two boys right there. I said, "I want to tell you something, and you listen to me straight. I don't want any more trouble out of you fellows tonight. I will do what I can, but I cannot do anything now. I have to make sure that the 225 are taken care of first. So please cooperate. Go over next to the hospital wall and be seated there until we're all done, and then I'll see what I can do."

They weren't too happy with that speech, but they obeyed. They went over and sat down. I asked Pastor Giao to get their names and other information and give it to me. Every time I returned with the ambulance, as soon as the security guard opened the gate for us and I drove the ambulance in, I looked off to my left and there were the young people—seven or eight of them. And like one person, they would jump to their feet just as the ambulance came in to see whether I would nod or shake my head. As the evening wore on, every time I came back in, I would shake my head, and they would sit back down.

About ten o'clock, as I drove back in, Pastor Giao came up to me, wringing his hands.

"Oh, Pastor Watts, we have a terrible problem. I don't know what happened, but somehow we notified two families that their names were included on the list, and they're here to go, but we've checked the list over, and their names aren't there. What are we going to do?"

"There's nothing I can do now, Pastor Giao," I said. There was one family of about seven, another of about eight—a total of fifteen or sixteen, if I remember correctly. They had been promised that they would be on the list, and told to be at the hospital at eight o'clock, ready to go. So there they were. I said, "Pastor Giao, you're going to have to give me their names and all the information about them." He provided me with the information. I stuffed it into my pocket, and we continued with another trip.

Later on in the evening, as I pulled in, one of the ambulances was still there, and I heard a lot of yelling and screaming and crying. I went over to Pastor Giao and said, "What's happening?"

He said, "Two young men have gotten into an ambulance. They've barricaded themselves in, and they refuse to get out. They are insisting that we take them to the airport."

That was the last thing we needed. That was one of the reasons we had decided to make the transfers after curfew, and why we had insisted that no one come to the hospital except the 225 who were on the list. The greatest fear I had during those evening hours was that someone would pull out a revolver or a machine gun and hold the entire group hostage. What would have happened then? We wanted to do everything possible to prevent that kind of a situation from developing. And now here were these two young men inside the ambulance. They refused to come out, and no one was going to go in after them.

I said, "Pastor Giao, this is your problem. You Vietnamese leaders are going to have to solve it. I can tell you one thing, though. We're going to suspend this whole evacuation right now until you and your Vietnamese brethren get those two young men out of that ambulance. There is no way we're taking them to the airport. They are not on the list, and they cannot go."

So Pastor Giao enlisted some of the younger men who were standing around. I'm telling you, that's another scene that I will not forget. Those men went into that ambulance and physically pulled those young men out, screaming, yelling, fighting, and kicking, and told them there was no way they could leave. Experiences like that leave an indelible impression on your mind.

More Trouble

By eleven or eleven-thirty we were down to practically the end of the run. I wanted to make sure that the last load included Pastor Giao and some of the key leaders. Up until this point we'd had little difficulty going from the hospital to the airport. I gathered Pastor Giao and the last of my group in the ambulance, and we left the hospital and turned onto the street. Bright lights hit us just as we entered the first main intersection. I screeched to a halt. An armored vehicle pulled up, and several soldiers with their guns pointed at us ordered me out of the ambulance. I got out and went over the side, and Pastor Giao got out. The officer, probably a captain, began speaking to Pastor Giao. Though I couldn't understand, I listened to the conversation for a while, and I became a little bit suspicious. Pretty soon Pastor Giao walked right past me, opened the door, looked toward the back of the ambulance, and barked out a few orders. Soon I saw packages, sacks, and purses begin making their way up to the front of the ambulance. Pastor Giao emerged with a rather large armful.

"I don't like this, Pastor Giao," I said. "I don't want you to do this."

"Pastor Watts, you let me take care of it."

I said, "No, I'm going to talk to the officer." I went over to the officer and told him that we had made these trips all during the night, that we had authorization for them from his government and my government, and we were not to have any kind of harassment. The last thing I wanted was a group of soldiers holding our group up for ransom. I told him that if he did not cooperate I would call the U.S. embassy, and American security guards would come out immediately to take care of the problem.

The officer talked to Pastor Giao, and I could tell by the tone of his voice that he was upset. I asked Pastor Giao what the officer said, but I don't think he translated very carefully. What I think he said was, "You tell that American to shut up and sit down. I'm dealing with you." But Pastor Giao translated it as, "Pastor Watts, he said to just go sit down in the ambulance and let us take care of it." So I went back and sat down, really upset. I saw Pastor Giao hand his bundle over to the officer.

When Pastor Giao got back in the ambulance, I said, "We're not leaving."

"What do you mean?"

"I'm not going to allow this to happen," I said firmly.

He then shared some good Asian philosophy with me. "Now, Pastor Watts, let's think of it this way. We're going to be leaving this country in a few hours, and all the money we have, whatever possessions we have right here at this time, will be of no use. But these men are not leaving. There is no way they can leave. If we help them at this time to prepare for their future, wouldn't we be doing a good thing?"

How do you like that?

"Still," I told Pastor Giao, "I don't like what is happening. I want you to talk to the officer and tell him that we have several more trips to make tonight, and I don't want any more of this." He talked to the officer. The officer listened. Then he snapped to attention, gave me a smart salute, and waved us on. We went on our way.

I dropped off Pastor Giao and the rest of our group, but I still had work to do. Remember the Chinese young people and those two families? So I went back to the gymnasium. I saw the M.P. and slipped in the side door. When I walked over to MacGregor's desk, he looked up at me, wondering why I was back. Weren't 225 enough? He didn't say that, but I knew he was thinking it.

I said, "Mr. MacGregor, I am terribly embarrassed." I kept using those words—"I am terribly embarrassed."

"What's the problem?" he asked.

"Inadvertently, two families—fifteen individuals altogether— were notified and promised that they would be allowed to leave. Their names were not on the manifest. I really have to have your help."

"Well," he said, "let me look at that letter of authorization again."

I pulled it out, and we looked at the wording. It didn't say 225! It just said, "The attached manifest."

He looked at the letter and said, "I don't see that we have a real problem. Where do you want them?"

I said, "Put them on my flight." So we added their names to that list.

I went back to the hospital, and there was that group of Chinese young people. As the security guard opened the gates, they all jumped to their feet, and this time I nodded. Immediately, they were over to the ambulance, and in a whisk they were inside. I turned the ambulance around and headed right back out the gate before the security guard could even close it. Those kids were singing and laughing and absolutely filled with excitement because their prayers had been answered.

Later, in the corridors of Glendale Adventist Medical Center, I bumped into one of those eight—a young lady by the name of Ei.

She lives in America, is married, has a child, and is working as a nurse.

After taking these young people to the airport, I came back for the other two families. We were able to get them into the ambulance and take them to the airport without any trouble.

By this time it was about one or one-thirty in the morning, and our group had grown to 225 plus. I don't really know how many we had there by this time. Dr. and Mrs. Weisseman were trying to make everyone as comfortable as possible. Unfortunately we had no place for the people to rest. Some of them were outside lying on the grass. Some were on the street with their little knapsacks. Others stretched on the gym floor with their heads on their belongings, trying to get a few hours of sleep. We were told by the processing officer that some might begin leaving Friday morning, possibly as early as five o'clock.

All through the night we heard the planes coming and going, and in the distance we could hear the heavy artillery. The city was literally under siege. There was no way of escape other than by air. As the guns kept going off in the distance, and as the jet planes kept taking off and landing, we kept wondering, When will our group be called? When will our group leave?

By one-thirty or two o'clock I was exhausted beyond the point of being able to stand or function. I turned to Romie and said, "Let's go back to the hospital one more time and try to get an hour or two of sleep." And we did.

The place was quite deserted now. Most of the medical staff and all the other expatriates had gone. They were out at the airport, waiting for their flights to be called. You can't imagine the emotions that swept over me as I walked through the corridors of that hospital.

We made our way across the alley and up the steps to the little apartment that I had. I said, "Romie, before I sleep, there's one thing I've got to do. I've got to have a shower, and I've got to wash these clothes." I'd worn them since Wednesday. So I kicked my shoes off and walked into the shower, fully clothed. I turned on that old spigot, and, as usual, all we had was cold water. Water coursed over me, and I picked up the soap. I was too tired to take off my clothes, so I washed my clothes and myself at the same time. Have you ever done that? I wasn't going to take the time to wash my body and my clothes separately, so I washed both thoroughly—or at least, I did my best. I wrung out my underwear and put it back on, and I hung my safari suit on a hanger. We had high ceilings with overhead fans. I climbed on a chair and worked out a little device so I could hang this outfit under the fan. I felt that if I could have two or three hours it would dry pretty well, even in that sultry climate. I went back and fell on my bed, totally exhausted, and immediately I was sound asleep.

All of a sudden, from that deep, sound sleep, I jumped up, startled. My heart must have been racing 120 or 130 beats a minute, and the adrenaline was flowing. I heard the guns going off in the distance. I heard the planes leaving, and all of a sudden, it hit me. They've called our flight! I just knew it. They'd called our flight, and we were at the hospital. Romie Gainer was awake, too, by now. I looked at my watch. It was three-thirty in the morning. I'd been asleep twenty minutes, but I was awake now.

Romie sat up. I said, "Romie, I feel uneasy. I think we'd better get back to the airport."

I got up, turned on the light, and went out into the living room to get my nice, fresh, clean, dry clothes. No such luck. After just twenty minutes, they were still sopping wet. I put them on, put on my shoes, and grabbed my shaving kit, which fortunately I happened to have in my attaché case. I put my Bible and my notes, along with my shaving kit, in my little attaché case, and we made our way down the steps, out into the corridor, and over to the ambulance. In the darkness of the night, we looked at the hospital for the very last time. I had been driving the ambulance back and forth to the airport through much of the night, but since this would most likely be our last trip, I asked one of our Vietnamese drivers to take us to the airport this time, and to stay with us for a few hours in case we should need the services of the ambulance again before our flight left. We got in the ambulance, the security guard opened the gate, and we left the hospital for good.

The Last Person Out

We made our way to the defense attaché complex. By this time both Romie and I were starving. Neither of us had eaten for many hours. We felt that we had a little time, so I said, "Let's grab some breakfast, because when we get started, we don't know how long it will be until we can eat." That breakfast was the last meal that I had for nearly thirty hours. I've made up for it since!

We went out to the airport. By this time it was five o'clock or five-thirty in the morning. As soon as I drove in, the very first person I saw, heading right for me, was Pastor Giao. He was wringing his hands. He came up to me and said, "Oh, Pastor Watts, we have a problem."

And I said, "What is it, Pastor Giao?"

"There's another family that we forgot to include on the list."

"Who is it this time?"

He said, "Do you remember Tran Chieu?"

"Of course, I know Tran Chieu."

Tran Chieu was a very successful Chinese businessman. He had a good business and resided in the Chinese section of Saigon. He was very active in the church. He was a member of the executive committee. He'd been helpful in building our church and school in Saigon, and he'd given much of his resources to support God's cause.

Pastor Giao said, "You know, as a member of the executive committee, this man could be in danger. Is there something that we could do to get him out of the country?"

I said, "Do you have any way of contacting him?"

"I think I can phone him."

"Well, then, you had better do it," I said. "You give me the names of his family members, and I'll see if I can get his name on the list."

So I went back to the gymnasium. It was about five-thirty. I walked in the side door, and I spoke to Mr. MacGregor. He'd been up all night. This time he didn't even bother to ask what I wanted. He just asked for the names, and I gave them to him. I'm not sure how many there were in the family—five or six, perhaps. It was not too large a number.

"Which manifest do you want them on?" he asked.

I said, "Put them on my flight."

I went back and told Pastor Giao, "Everything is all set. We have arranged for Tran Chieu and his family to leave if they choose to leave. But you must contact them."

He said, "I'll contact them." Somehow, he found his way to a telephone.

Now, I want you to picture this as if you were Tran Chieu. He is sound asleep. At six o'clock in the morning the telephone rings. The voice on the other end says, "Tran Chieu?"

"Yes."

"This is Giao. Arrangements have been made for you and your family to leave the country. Pastor Watts and I will meet you at the gate of the airport at 7:00 A.M. Be there, sharp." And the phone is hung up.

Now what would you do if you were Tran Chieu? I'm sure he looked at his house. It was beautifully furnished. I'm sure he thought of his shop, his factory, his employees, his business, his income. Everything he had, everything he owned, was right there. At that moment that man had to make a decision. I'm not sure he even had time to consult with his wife. Should we take the offer and go? Should we take our chances and stay? If we go, we don't know what the future holds for us. If we stay, it is uncertain as well. He had to make a very difficult decision.

At seven o'clock he was there at the airport gate. Pastor Giao and the ambulance driver and I were there at seven o'clock, too, but somehow we missed each other. To this day, we still don't know how it happened, but miraculously, Tran Chieu and his family drove right up to the entrance and entered with no problem at all. They went right through the barricaded area, past the security guard, to the inside of the airport, where he met our people.

Meanwhile, Pastor Giao and I were outside the gate trying to find him. By this time hundreds of people were beginning to gather around the gate. The first of our group had already left on the evacuation flight. I told Pastor Giao, "We cannot wait any longer. Apparently Mr. Chieu has decided not to leave. Let's go back in."

Just as our driver was getting ready to turn the ambulance around and go back into the airport, a security guard came over—an officer. He stopped us and asked Pastor Giao for his authorization to enter the airport. Suddenly I realized we were in real trouble. I had left the manifest with all of the authorizations behind with Romie Gainer and Harvey Rudisaile and the group at the airport. Pastor Giao and I had gone outside the gate without it. The security guard said to Pastor Giao, "You cannot leave Saigon. There's no way that I can permit you to go through the gates into that airport. You're going to have to get out of the ambulance."

We argued with him. I tried to convince him that all during

the night we had been bringing all these people through the gates without any difficulty. I pled with him. Pastor Giao pled with him. But the officer was adamant, and Pastor Giao was forced to get out of the ambulance.

He got out with a very heavy heart, I can assure you. I think that at that time he was convinced that perhaps he would have to remain behind. His wife and children were gone. They had left for Guam several days earlier with Don Roth's group.

I said, "Pastor Giao, I will go back in and get the manifest, and I'll be back here in a short time to pick you up."

He said, "Pastor Watts, look at the traffic. There's no way that you can get there and back in a short period of time. And look at the people out here. There's no way you could find me.

I said, "Pastor Giao, listen to me. You stay right here. Don't move from this spot. I will go in, get the manifest, and come back and get you."

As I got into the ambulance, I thought, *After all this—after all that we have gone through, to think that there might be a possibility that Pastor Giao would not make this flight!* I was determined to find a way, somehow.

By this time, the hospital staff was on duty. I asked the ambulance driver to take us into the airport area. We went inside the gate and made our way through the security check. He had a security pass, and they weren't going to stop me, since I was an American. And then the driver had an idea. He stopped the ambulance and pulled off to the side.

In broken English, he said, "Let Pastor Giao drive the ambulance. They won't stop him if he's driving the ambulance."

Why hadn't I thought of that? "Of course," I said. "Let's turn the ambulance around."

So the driver made a U-turn right there in that busy intersection, and we made our way back through the gate to the very spot outside where we had left Pastor Giao.

There were hundreds of people milling around by this time. Pastor Giao was wearing navy blue trousers and a light-yellow, short-sleeve shirt. I still remember exactly what he was wearing. We went back to the same spot, but Pastor Giao was nowhere in sight. I looked all around. I couldn't see him anywhere. We looked this direction and that direction, but neither of us could see him.

Suddenly the driver motioned to me and said, "Look." About a quarter of a mile down the road was a figure walking toward the hospital. It was Pastor Giao. I recognized him even at that distance. We jumped into the ambulance, and the driver floored it. Seconds later we screeched to a halt. The driver got out and explained to Pastor Giao what we had in mind. Pastor Giao got in and sat in the driver's seat. The driver took off his I.D. tag with his picture and put it on Pastor Giao's shirt. "You drive," he said. "I'll go back to the hospital from here, and I'll come back later for the ambulance."

Pastor Giao made another U-turn, and we headed back toward the airport. Suddenly, he stopped. I wondered what was going on.

"Pastor Watts," he said, "this will never work. This will never work."

"What do you mean? What else can we do?"

"What happens if we go back to the checkpoint and that same security officer is there and he sees that I have on this false I.D.? If he forces me out of the ambulance again under these circumstances, there is no way that you or anyone else can ever get me back through those gates."

"Pastor Giao, I'm sure this is the only solution," I said.

"I think I have a better one," he replied.

"What is it?"

"I think that the only way this will succeed is if you drive the ambulance. They won't stop you."

I said, "I'll give it a try."

We quickly switched places. I got into the driver's seat, and he moved over to the right side. I made a final left turn and headed toward the airport. As we neared the gate I slowed down. I wanted the traffic to clear between us and the car in front. I allowed about a hundred feet to clear in front of us. When the last vehicle had passed the barbed-wire security checkpoint into the airbase, I began to accelerate. I was determined that one way or another we were going to get through.

As the ambulance picked up speed, I turned to Pastor Giao and said, "Turn the other way. Look the other direction." Pastor Giao turned to the right. The guardhouse was on the left. As we approached, I looked to the left, and there checking the vehicles, was the same security guard that had just forced Pastor Giao out of the ambulance. But he was talking to someone. He turned around as we drove by, but by that time the ambulance was through. We were inside now, in territory that was being guarded by the Vietnamese and U.S. military. Pastor Giao slumped down in his seat, shaking. I put my hand on his shoulder and said, "We're on our way now. We're on our way."

We went out to the area where people were exiting for the airplanes. There we found that Tran Chieu and his family had arrived and that others of our group were leaving.

Perhaps you remember that we had been told that both of the Weissemans would be on the same flight. Jean and her group went out to board the airplane. George was supposed to be right behind her, but for some reason the government had other plans. Another group of people had a higher priority than ours. After Jean's group passed through the final checkpoint, another group was inserted, and the airplane was filled with Jean's group and this other group. They closed the doors, and there was Jean in the airplane, but no George. She took off for the Philippines. A few moments later George and two or three other groups boarded their plane and took off.

Then the rest of our group began to leave. The last of our groups, before mine, included Rudisaile, Branson, and Gainer. By now our group was relatively small. The rest had left. Then Gainer and his group left. You cannot imagine the sensation I felt at that time. I felt so terribly alone. All the others had gone. Our group was now the last.

Gainer's plane lifted off at eleven-thirty Friday morning. Finally, at about noon, they called for our group. We were the last. Pastor Giao, Le Huu, and some of the other leaders and employees with their families boarded the buses. We made our way out to the tarmac, and there we got off the buses and waited. The planes had been leaving about every twenty or thirty minutes, but for some reason there was a delay at this point. We waited and waited. Twelve o'clock came. Then twelve-thirty and one o'clock. All kinds of thoughts began to go through my mind. No air traffic. No airplanes. No sounds of jets, either landing or taking off. Fear began to grip my heart.

I thought, *What has happened? Has the government capitulated? Are we now prisoners of the North Vietnamese and just don't know it yet? Has the president called off the evacuation?* These were the various thoughts that were going through my mind. I was the only American in that group of about 180. I felt so alone!

I kept looking into the eastern sky. There were white fluffy clouds, but my eyes were searching, and my ears were listening, for an airplane. Suddenly, I saw a little reflection, a sparkle in the sun. Could that be it? I watched as it went behind a cloud, and when it emerged, I could see that it was an aircraft. As it came closer, I recognized it as a large C-141 transport. You cannot imagine the intensity with which I watched this silver bird coming in closer, closer, closer. Soon I heard the jet engine, and I watched as the plane began its descent. I watched as it touched down on the runway. I watched that plane every minute, every second, as it made its way out to the end of the runway and then turned around and came back. It pulled up right in front of where we were standing.

As the plane swung around, its rear hatches opened up, and an air force officer came out and motioned with his hand. Like one person, those of us who were standing by the buses rushed out and swarmed into that airplane. It didn't take more than a few seconds. Then the doors slammed shut, the plane made its way out to the end of the runway, and in a few moments the pilot gave it the full throttle, and those great jet engines began to move the aircraft down the runway. We took off.

I looked around. All around me were my Vietnamese brothers and sisters. Some I had never seen before, yet I felt very close to them at that moment. There was crying, sobbing, laughing, smiles—a wide range of emotions. The plane was carrying us to Guam.

The Miracle of 410

The Seventh-day Adventist mission in Guam did an unbelievable job of providing for us. Our people were scattered throughout seven or eight camps all over that island. It took a couple of days to find them all and get their names. When we got the total count, we found that instead of 225 people, 410 persons had left Vietnam during that week in our groups!

I was still wearing the same safari suit. The dear sisters in Guam, bless their hearts, took pity on me and found some clothes in their Community Service supplies that they let me use during the days that I was there. And they washed my safari suit for me. I arrived early Sabbath morning, and I left on Tuesday afternoon, so for several days I had clean clothes, for which I was thankful.

We contacted the General Conference and Loma Linda University. The university performed a magnanimous act. As an organization, representatives said to the United States government, "We will guarantee these 410 people that are coming our way."

On Tuesday, April 29, I left Guam for the United States to make preparations for the Vietnamese who would be arriving in just a few days. I put my safari suit back on, and with about four hundred other Vietnamese I boarded a plane for Travis Air Force Base, where I was met by a General Conference representative.

He said, "The first thing we've got to do is to make some contact with key government officials."

I said, "What do you mean? How can I go like this? I've got to buy some proper clothes."

"Hey, look," he said. "You're in California now. Anything goes." A few years later when I moved to California, I realized that he was right. So we contacted various government officials to let them know what was happening and who was coming.

Then I boarded a flight for Ontario, near Loma Linda, California. I was met there by Vern Small and taken out to Loma Linda, where our oldest daughter Edie lived. She and her husband were students at Loma Linda University.

Vern asked, "Do you want us to get you a motel?"

"No," I said, "I'll stay with my daughter."

Bear in mind that during this time our families did not know what was happening to us. When we arrived in Guam, word got out to our parents, to our wives, and our families. But there was a time when even my wife did not have a clue as to what was happening to me. There was even a time when she wondered whether I had gotten out of the country or I had had to stay behind.

At any rate, I said to Vern, "I don't want to stay in a motel. I want to be with my daughter." So they drove me out to her apartment. As we approached, I saw her seated at the window in her little dining area, so I said, "Drive on by; I want to surprise her."

Vern drove a little past the apartment. I got out, slipped around, and knocked on the door. My daughter opened the door, and there was her dad. She burst into tears as she rushed into my arms.

"Dad," she said, "I've just been reading *U.S. News & World Report* about the evacuation, and we haven't heard anything about what happened to our missionaries or to you."

I comforted her, "Edie, it's all over. We're safe. We're home."

Two days later the 410 Vietnamese arrived from Guam. Loma Linda University opened its heart and its homes and its facilities, and did everything humanly possible to help. We are deeply indebted to them.

I have just shared with you my experience, as viewed through my eyes. Others would give you a different version, because they all experienced it and saw it through different eyes. I want you to know how much I appreciate the contribution they have made to the cause of God. We are grateful for the leadership and for the contribution that the Vietnamese have made here in this country. I know that some in this country wondered why it was necessary to bring these people to our land, but I'm here to tell you that I believe with all my heart that their lives have been a blessing to us. I want to pay a special tribute to Pastor Giao and his wife, who sacrificed so much. These two people have given of themselves twenty-four hours a day, seven days a week, twelve months out of the year, to help their people. They've given of their resources. They've opened up their home. They've had dozens of refugees live with them until they could get established and resettled. That is a positive testimony of Christianity in action. The Giaos have personally sponsored through their church no less than four hundred boat people. Many of them have come to live with their family. And almost two hundred of those four hundred became Seventh-day Adventists! They have an organized Vietnamese church, 90 percent of whom are these so-called boat people!

What's happened to the church in Vietnam since? The ones that left were predominantly those whose lives were in danger, which meant that the vast majority of our employees remained behind. Our pastors, our teachers, our colporteurs, many of our publishing leaders remained behind, because in the judgment of the Vietnamese leaders their lives were not endangered. After the

North Vietnamese took over the government, the remaining Vietnamese church and lay leaders met together and organized, and one of our pastors was selected as the president; another one was selected as secretary; another was named as the treasurer. Now these men endeavored to carry on the work of God under very difficult and trying circumstances. There is still an interest in Christianity. The churches that have been allowed to function are full. The church in Vietnam is still giving witness to the grace of God and His ultimate plan for His people and this planet.

Epilogue: Thirteen Years Later

In March 1988 I returned to Vietnam with several colleagues, including Pastor Giao and Pastor Gainer, at the invitation of the Socialist Republic of Vietnam (SRVN). As president of the Adventist Development and Relief Agency (ADRA), I undertook this fact-finding trip to meet with government officials, visit several hospitals and clinics, and get a firsthand look at the critical needs the country was facing at the time.

As our flight from Bangkok to Hanoi was descending, bad weather kept us from seeing the ground at all. The flaps had been extended and the wheels lowered when all of a sudden the pilot applied power, pulled up the flaps and landing gear, and proceeded to climb. After circling for about fifteen minutes, the pilot told us that we would not be landing in Hanoi. The runway was closed because of an accident—an Air Vietnam flight coming in from Saigon had apparently just crashed on landing. We returned to Thailand, refueling in Ubon.

The next morning we again went to the airport, checked in, cleared immigration and security, and then waited and waited. When we finally left, the flight was uneventful, but as we landed in the drizzle at Hanoi, we glimpsed the plane that had crashed the day before. Fortunately, there had been no fatalities.

Epilogue: Thirteen Years Later

On our arrival we had to complete quite a bit of paperwork in order to clear immigration and customs. The airport was small and old. Armed guards kept pacing back and forth on a balcony, surveying carefully all that was taking place below. After we cleared customs, we were met by Mr. Quan from the American desk of the Ministry of Foreign Affairs, who was to be our guide. He helped us process our customs papers, which were quite complicated and detailed. We had some trouble collecting our luggage because several pieces still had the previous day's tags on them, and we no longer had those stubs. The workers were very careful to see that everything was done properly.

When we finally collected all our luggage, we loaded it into a van for the twenty-five mile trip into Hanoi. It was an interesting drive through the countryside and past little towns. First we looked out on rice-paddy fields; then, as we got closer to Hanoi, we saw the vendors selling flowers and bread, etc. It was difficult to see the residual effects of the war, except out in the fields, where we could see craters from the bombing.

We were certainly impressed by the ubiquitous bicycles. There are 1.1 million bicycles in Hanoi alone! All motor vehicles are government owned except those owned by foreign services, embassies, and business firms located in Hanoi. At times traffic was quite heavy—a lot of hustle and bustle.

It was a dark, drizzly day—the kind that never gives a positive impression of a city. At one time Hanoi must have been a very beautiful city. It has a number of parks and several lakes. Our hotel was located at the edge of the city. The rooms seemed bleak, sparsely furnished, and dimly lit. Because we had been delayed, we were completely off schedule, and it was impossible to meet any government leaders that day. We were anxious to get into our work, but it couldn't be helped.

The next morning we met with the vice-director of the North American office, Ministry of Foreign Affairs. We shared an overview of ADRA's background and experience, the activities in which we are involved, and our willingness to assist Vietnam. The vice-director was very concerned about the MIA issue and the normalization of relations with the United States government. I took great pains to explain that we were an international humanitarian organization and that we could not speak for the United States government. We asked what their greatest needs were, and he shared a number of areas common to most developing countries—health care, medicines, medical supplies, nutrition, clean water, agricultural assistance, etc.

In the afternoon we met with the director of the Department for Economic Cooperation under the Ministry of Foreign Affairs. He outlined the economic difficulties that the country was facing, and he said that the course of action they had been pursuing for the last thirteen years was not working. They needed to make drastic changes in their government policies to encourage foreign investment. Any help we could provide, from a humanitarian standpoint, would take pressure off the government, because all services were provided by the government—housing, jobs, education, health care, etc.

We were scheduled to leave Hanoi for Ho Chi Minh City (Saigon) on Sunday. However, when we arrived at the airport, we found many other people trying to do the same thing. Because of the air accident, they were short on aircraft, and there was a backlog of passengers. So, even though we had top priority, others ahead of us had higher priority and had been waiting longer. We had no choice but to return to Hanoi. It was frustrating, for it seemed like another wasted day.

Mr. Quan helped us get our tickets rewritten at the airport office, and we were able to arrange for a flight on Wednesday. It was quite an ordeal and took a good deal of time, energy, and stops at many different offices. He then did what he could to arrange for us to meet with more government officials. On Monday and Tuesday we met with several officials and were able to visit a few hospitals.

During the war, Bach Mai Hospital, the largest in Hanoi, had been hit by B-52 bombers in a bombing raid. Our tour was pretty much as I expected. The hospital was dark and dingy, with wet floors and antiquated equipment. Most of the equipment had been donated by an American group in 1973 following the cease-fire, and much of it was no longer functioning properly. Supplies were woefully inadequate, and the hospital was in desperate need of medicines. In the ICU ward the only equipment that worked was a couple of IVs. And it was very dirty.

We then visited a moderate-sized hospital where the conditions were much the same. The beds had no mattresses, and equipment was virtually nonexistent. I marveled at the ability to treat patients with these meager facilities. As in many Asian hospitals, there was the problem of extended families gathering at the hospital. Children, parents, and other relatives were all gathered outside, by the beds, in the halls, and on the stairways. They had brought their food and blankets and slept on the floor. It created havoc for maintenance and sanitation, but apparently there was no way to get around this.

We were taken to a rural clinic on the outskirts of town. The weather was drizzling, and the roads were muddy as we made our way to this little village dispensary. Three nurses worked there, primarily taking care of accident cases and delivering babies. They did not have any cleaning equipment. The lab consisted of a little alcohol and a small tray of antiquated instruments.

After visiting these institutions we were convinced that anything we could send, regardless of how meager or worn, would be better than anything they had even in their finest hospital. The problem isn't in getting the equipment. It's in finding the funds to pay for the shipments.

After these visits, we met with the minister of health. I read a statement indicating that, on behalf of ADRA, we wished to show our good faith by providing a small initial gift of a shipment sent within thirty days that would include good used medical instruments, medicines, medical supplies, and other commodities. As I read this statement, the minister jumped to his feet, grasped my hand with both of his, and kept shaking my hand and thanking us over and over on behalf of the ministry and the people. We spoke of other possibilities, and he expressed a desire to work more closely with the West in being brought up to date in medical training and research. (The shipment was sent. Sadly, the minister of health was later killed in an air accident.)

We left Hanoi for the airport at a quarter of six Wednesday morning. During the entire time we were in Hanoi, we never saw the sun shine—not once. It seemed like everything was always muddy. We were looking forward to going south to a warmer and sunnier climate. Even though it was still dark and still raining, we were surprised at the amount of traffic along the road, mostly bicycles, at that time of morning. The airport was already crowded. Mr. Quan helped us check in.

We boarded our Soviet-built jet at 7:20, and at 7:30, before most of the passengers had even found their seats, the pilot cranked up the engine and began to taxi out. This must have inspired everyone, because by the time the plane reached the runway, everyone was in place. The overhead luggage racks were not enclosed, so had there been any turbulence, everything would have come flying down on the passengers. The baggage was placed unsecured in the back of the aircraft. We were not asked to buckle up. There was no such thing as a nonsmoking section. The service was casual and relaxed, to say the least.

Many memories flooded through my mind as we descended into Saigon. I recognized much of the countryside. We flew over the C-5A crash site. The remnants of the war were still visible: guns in place, old aircraft, military vehicles, and trucks lined up and rusting out. I disembarked first and stood at the bottom of the steps, waiting for Pastor Giao so we could walk together. As he came down, I put my arm around him and said, "Welcome home, Pastor Giao." It was a very moving experience for both of us. We spoke of the stressful, heart-wrenching circumstances under which we had left that exact spot thirteen years before.

At the terminal we were met by Madame Hao, the protocol officer for the Ministry of Foreign Affairs. She gave us a warm, friendly welcome. We ate a light breakfast at the airport restaurant, then loaded our bags in a van and were driven to the government guest house. It was a large compound with high walls and a big gate. It must have been a beautiful embassy complex at one time. We were staying in two of the large French villas where the government houses VIPs and officials of other countries when they come for state visits. Shortly thereafter we left for an overnight trip to the city of Can Tho.

On the trip in the van to Can Tho we were taking pictures and video. Once in a while Madame Hao would hear the shutter clicking, turn to us, and say, "No, you must not take a picture of that."

As we passed some fruit stands selling luscious-looking mangoes, she ordered the driver to stop while she purchased some, for it was to be a long drive. As she left the car, Pastor Giao noticed that we were parked directly across the street from a large Seventh-day Adventist Chinese church. We jumped out and began taking pictures. When I walked inside the courtyard, a young man came up, recognized me, and asked if we wanted to see the pastor. I knew this was not the appropriate time, so I said, "No, no. We will come back in two or three days," and we quickly made our way back to the van.

We had not gone more than two or three blocks when we looked out the window, and there on a motorcycle was the pastor, Frankie Lee, with this young man riding behind him. He waved at us, and we cautiously waved back, trying not to let Madame Hao know what we were doing. He followed us for quite some time. When we stopped at a major intersection, he could not help himself. He drove up next to us and stuck his head in the window to shake hands with Pastor Giao who was sitting between the driver and Madame Hao. Pastor Giao acted surprised and said, "Hello, how are you?" in English. We in the back seat put our fingers to our lips and shook our heads and motioned for him to leave. But he would not leave. He followed us for some time. We were confident that within a matter of hours he would have the word out through the Adventist community that we had arrived in the south.

As we sped along to Can Tho, we enjoyed the countryside. The large Mekong Delta is flat, very fertile, and productive. We witnessed a great deal of river activity and had to take ferries across the large rivers. The ferries were jammed with people, trucks, buses, vehicles, bicycles, motorbikes, etc. We saw many children working as vendors, selling cigarettes, candy, fruit, and other goods. Several of them were Amerasians.

The next morning we visited the school of medicine and the teaching hospital in Can Tho. Following this we proceeded to a small community hospital quite close to where Pastor Giao's father had lived for so many years. We traveled about eight kilometers along a dirt road and then walked the rest of the way along the river to the church that Pastor Giao's father had raised up so many years before.

In the back of the church was a room where Pastor Giao's eighty-six-year-old stepmother still lived. As she came out of that little room, very small and fragile, she saw her stepson for the first time in thirteen years. They threw their arms around each other, and their tears intermingled. She spoke tenderly to him, patting his hair and touching his face. Then they walked behind the church so Pastor Giao could visit his father's gravesite for the first time. The rest of us had purchased some flowers at the previous village. We gave them to him now to place at the grave. He walked up, stood for a few moments, then burst into tears. He bowed his head and spoke in Vietnamese. He knelt before his father's grave, and with anguish offered a prayer. Many villagers had gathered around. Some were friends, some relatives, others just onlookers. They stood aside and waited respectfully.

After a few moments Pastor Giao stood and expressed public appreciation to the officials for making it possible for him to make this pilgrimage. We put our arms around him as he spoke of his father's great influence and the hope of the resurrection. Then we returned to the church, where Pastor Giao greeted the members. It was a joyful experience for them to visit with their former church leader. When we were through, his stepmother bid him a tearful farewell, and we proceeded back to the van. We returned to Can Tho to meet with some officials, then journeyed back to Ho Chi Minh City.

On Friday Madame Hao arranged for a private car and driver for Pastor Giao so that he could visit relatives and friends. Many people in the United States had asked him to bring letters and money to help their families in Vietnam. In each place he was greeted with surprise and many tears. The people were amazed that he could come and visit with them. Many of the people kept touching him, as if they couldn't believe he was really there. One eighty-two-year-old lady cried and said she wanted to talk to him, but she was so surprised that she couldn't remember what to say.

When he stopped at the mission office and asked the driver to take a picture of him in front of the office sign, someone inside heard him, and suddenly the office staff rushed out to see him and embrace him. The pastor spoke to them of the importance of being faithful in continuing to lead the work. He told them that they were not forgotten. Each place he visited, the people were so anxious to talk to him. They begged him to stay longer—just a few minutes more. It was very hard for him to leave, but he could not stay, for he had many people to visit. It was a long, emotional day for Pastor Giao.

While the pastor was taking care of this business, the rest of us met with several government officials. On our way to the compound for lunch, we were able to take a quick drive through the city so we could again see many of the familiar sights. We drove past the former U.S. embassy. We passed the Palace Hotel, where we had held our midyear union committee meeting in May 1974. A flood of memories swept over us as we drove past shops that we had browsed in and sidewalks where we had once strolled.

Unfortunately, when Pastor Giao left on his errands, we had not discussed the time when he would be returning. We should have asked him to leave his passport with us, because Madame Hao needed it in order to change the police and security permit for our stay, which was to expire that day. When she came to pick us up for our appointments after lunch and he had not yet returned, she was quite concerned. As we drove out, she gave instructions to the security guard at the gate that should Pastor Giao arrive, he was to meet us at one of the two hospitals we were going to visit.

We finished our tour at around five o'clock in the evening and returned to our residence, only to discover that Pastor Giao still had not returned. By this time Madame Hao was really concerned and somewhat upset since she was responsible for our security. We went over our schedule for the following day, which was Sabbath, and found that our chances of being able to go to church were limited because the passport problem had to be resolved before we could go anywhere. Over supper we tried to figure out a way to meet with our people. Perhaps we could see them at an afternoon service. Just as we were finishing up, Pastor Giao returned. We told him of the problem and that we probably would not be able to take care of it in time to attend church. He felt upset that he had not thought to leave his passport.

Yet on Sabbath morning one of the most beautiful turns of events took place. I believe God provided a miracle. Madame Hao arrived at the villa at 7:15, picked up our passports, and took them to the Ministry of Foreign Affairs, where two additional days were to be approved. Even though she promised to be back as soon as possible, it appeared as though any hope of our attending church was in vain, for Sabbath School started at 8:00 A.M. and church at 9:00. However, at 8:45 we gathered at the main villa so we could leave immediately should she return in time. We visited together, frequently looking at our watches. At 9:20 we saw the van. We sprang up, jumped into the van, and drove toward the headquarters church. Madame Hao told us that it had taken a fair amount of explaining to her superiors to extend our stay. We were elated. It was hard to believe we were actually on our way to meet with our Vietnamese brothers and sisters with the official blessing of the government!

As the driver pulled into the familiar church courtyard, some of the members spotted us, and within seconds, a group came outside the church to greet us officially. Looking out, I saw a number of familiar faces. We sat there rather dazed for a second or two; then we jumped out of the van and began taking pictures and shaking hands. The preaching service got underway. The speaker that morning was Pastor Son, the mission president. The church was packed, but they cleared a back pew for us by the door, and we walked in and sat down.

When Pastor Giao had met with the mission leaders on Friday, he had indicated to them that we were going to try to attend church, and he asked that every effort be put forth to avoid any emotional display. Apparently, the word got out, but you could tell by the tears that welled up in people's eyes that they were thrilled to see us, especially their dear friend, Pastor Giao.

At the end of the sermon we were introduced and asked to stand. Following the closing prayer a formal picture was taken of the entire group, as is traditional in Asian countries when special guests arrive. Then we were able to shake hands with the people and talk with them. It was such a joy to see some of our former workers. They looked a little more gaunt, and it was apparent that they had had a difficult time, but their faith and courage seemed to be good, and they were giving positive leadership.

As we were greeting old friends, I spoke with one Vietnamese layman of the experience I had had in 1975 at that very church during the mission constituency session. A cement block fell off the roof and hit the back of my head with a glancing blow. I was rushed to the hospital, had the wound sutured, and returned to the session. The delegates couldn't believe that I was able to return, and they applauded as I stepped onto the platform to reconvene the nominating committee. I told them that a union president needed two qualifications—a hard head and a soft heart—and I hoped that I qualified on both accounts. This brother reminded me of that statement, and we had a good laugh.

After nearly all the group had left, two ladies came and sat beside me: Mrs. Hoang and her daughter. The daughter pleaded with me to help reunite her family. The father, Pastor Hoang, and three of the children had been able to escape from Vietnam a number of years earlier, with the hope that the mother and three other children would be able to join them soon after they were established in the United States. At this time, Pastor Hoang was serving as an associate pastor in the Carmichael church in Sacramento, and the three children were studying in San Jose. Mrs. Hoang and the other three children had made application for reunification, but the case had been dragging on for a number of years.

I told the daughter that I would be meeting with the minister of external affairs before leaving the country and that I would personally take up the matter with him and appeal for his help in an urgent request for his influence in reuniting the family. Mrs. Hoang could not speak English, but her smile showed her appreciation. What a heartbreaking situation!

After the picture taking and handshaking began slowing down, I went up to Pastor Son, and we had a few moments alone. I put my arm around him and said, "Pastor Son, I want you to know that we think of you and pray for you often. God will give you the courage and wisdom necessary to lead His people in this country. Be of good courage. God will give you strength." Tears welled up in his eyes, and he laid his head on my shoulder as a son would with a father. I gave him a squeeze and grabbed his hand and shook it warmly, and then we had to leave. As we rode back to the villa, we recounted the tremendous inspiration that had come to us during the few moments we had had with our people during the time of worship and following the service.

After lunch we were met by Madame Hao, who escorted us downtown to the office of Ambassador Bong, the minister of external affairs for southern Vietnam and the highest-ranking party official in the south. Ambassador Bong was very warm and spoke with animation and emotion. He asked how we had enjoyed our stay in Vietnam, if we had been able to see what we wished, and if we felt that our trip was successful. We expressed deep gratitude for the invitation of the Vietnamese government to visit the country and for the kindness extended to us by our hosts. We said that we were impressed with the commitment the people had to improving their quality of life, and that we wanted to join with them in a partnership role to help alleviate some of the suffering and hardships that we'd seen. We had a good dialogue.

Then I told him that I had debated whether to even bring up the next topic, but I felt that he was a compassionate man with great concern for the people of his country. I told him that I was seeking counsel about the family of one of our employees in the United States. Then I told him about the Pham Minh Hoang family and how they had been separated for so long. He responded positively. He examined the documents I had with me. He asked me to write him a letter about the situation before leaving the country. We were encouraged. This letter and others were sent, and in May 1989, Mrs. Pham Minh Hoang and family departed Vietnam for the United States.

On the way back to the villa, we asked if we could stop at our Chinese church, which we had seen on our first day in the city when we stopped at the fruit stand. We hoped that we could meet a few of the workers and members there. We parked in front, walked through the gate, and noticed that a youth meeting was in progress. We took a number of pictures and then slipped in the back and sat down. The facility looked very nice. The inside had recently been painted. After about thirty minutes we asked Frankie Lee, the pastor, who had been one of our students at Southeast Asia Union College in Singapore, if it would be possible for us to break into the program for a few moments so that we could take a group photograph of the people that were there. He said they would be happy to do it and made an announcement. They quickly got things set up, and we got a group photo of the young people, a number of adults and church leaders, and the pastoral staff. After the pictures were taken, I called Frankie aside and said, "Frankie, we are very proud of the leadership you have given this church. I know that it has been difficult, and you have been lonely, but I want you to know that many of us have been thinking about you and have prayed for you and the members. Next Sabbath, give your people special greetings and let them know that the world church is praying for them, that we want them to be faithful and courageous."

Tears welled up in his eyes, and he found it difficult to speak. About that time Madame Hao motioned that we needed to leave, and Frankie quickly rushed over, shook her hand, and thanked her for bringing our delegation to the church. As we walked toward the gate I could see that he was having a difficult time with his emotions. I said, "I want to have one more picture," and I went back and stood by Frankie, put my arm around him, and spoke to him once more. I shook his hand another time, and then we left.

Back at the villa, we had sundown worship in my room. We thanked the Lord for the tremendous blessing that had come to us on this very unusual and special Sabbath. We felt sure that our presence had been a morale booster to the leaders and members, knowing that the world church was with them and that they were not all alone.

After supper we took a pedicab to the heart of the city, where the tourist area is located. We had visited this place many times before. It was interesting to see the familiar sights and walk through the streets again. We stopped at a rooftop restaurant and had an orange drink while overlooking the city. We reminisced—remembering what had been and thinking of what might have been.

On Sunday morning we visited the Christian and Missionary Alliance church. We had deliberately asked to visit a number of churches because we did not want to single out the Adventist Church. The church was packed that Sunday. We took photos and visited with a few of the local people. Standing on the periphery, we noticed several of our Adventist believers who had known that we would be visiting the C&MA church. We then left to visit a Catholic cathedral in the heart of the city.

Mass was underway at the beautiful old cathedral. We noticed that it was quite well filled. There were four masses in the morning and one in the afternoon. After the service, we took a few photos and looked around. Then we returned to our villa.

It was time to say goodbye to Madame Hao. We told her that she had gone the second mile for us as our guide. We took some pictures and bade her farewell. Pastor Giao set off to visit several members and to make some purchases for those who needed special help, including the purchase of a generator for the church. The rest of us spent the afternoon sightseeing, packing, and finishing up some projects.

We were soon on our way to Tan Son Nhut airport to catch our flight to Bangkok. En route from the villa, we took the main street to the airport, which took us by the compound where we had been building the new Saigon Adventist Hospital prior to the fall of the country. Madame Hao had not been willing for us to stop and visit the facility. However, a new protocol officer was with us now who was not aware of what she had said, and I asked the driver to stop. We immediately jumped out without saying much and proceeded into the hospital complex. Very little construction had been done on the hospital since we had left in 1975. At that time the building had been approximately 75 percent completed. Now we saw that the elevator shafts were still open. The ceilings were not in—just the cement slab for the floor above—and the wires and plumbing were bare and exposed. Nevertheless, the building was being used as a hospital.

We met briefly with the associate medical director and some others of the staff, giving the impression that we were looking over the hospital to ascertain whether we would be in a position to give them any assistance with medical supplies or equipment. But the real purpose of our visit was to see what had happened there during the intervening years. We left feeling a bit sad, realizing that not much had been accomplished since April 1975.

We proceeded to the airport, checked in, and were extremely pleased to see that a large number of our friends had come to say goodbye. The departure was delayed, giving us an opportunity for some fine visits with key church leaders and other members.

Soon we were called to board the bus that would take us out to an Air France 747 jet, which would soon be winging its way to Bangkok. It was very difficult for our friends to see us walk through the doors leading to immigration and customs, not knowing when they would see us again. We were the first real official contact that they had had with church leadership since 1975. We looked up on the observation deck and saw these very special people waving their handkerchiefs and saying farewell. It was truly with mixed emotions that we boarded the aircraft, anxious to be on our way toward home, but saddened that we were leaving behind a portion of our hearts.

Epilogue: Thirty Years Later

It hardly seems possible that more than thirty years have elapsed since we experienced that most traumatic week of our lives, and much has taken place in the intervening years.

Epilogue 1 ("Thirteen Years Later") tells of our short trip back to Vietnam following the fall of Saigon—the trip that we made in 1988 at the invitation of the government. On that brief visit we were able to make some excellent contacts, not only with government officials but also with many of our church leaders.

Little did we realize at the time that the visits we were able to have with various officials at the top levels of government would open the doors for more activity and involvement with different government ministries and local communities.

The Socialist Republic of Vietnam (SRVN) concurred with our request to open an ADRA office in the country. Exploratory visits were made after our visit in 1988 with the Tidwells—Dennis and Lila Tidwell were working in Cambodia at the time, and Dennis's father, Charles, was also assisting with the ADRA work in Cambodia. The Tidwells made a number of trips into Saigon (now renamed Ho Chi Minh City), and it was agreed that this city was where we would begin our operations as an agency. Office space was secured and an apartment found; Dennis and Lila

Tidwell moved into Ho Chi Minh City and established an ADRA office in the country.

ADRA was one of the first international nongovernmental organizations (NGOs) to establish a presence in Vietnam following the capitulation of the South to North Vietnam.

Granted, it was a very humble beginning, but it was a beginning. Shortly after the Tidwells arrived in Ho Chi Minh City, a young lady in the headquarters church was enlisted to assist them—a single mom who was dedicated to the work of the church and who found in herself a very compassionate heart for her people who were suffering and living under most difficult conditions. Her name was Kim Mai. She served very faithfully under the ADRA leader for many years. Kim Mai was able to develop very good relationships with key government officials and, of course, was an invaluable assistant in bridging the gulf between key government ministries and the foreigners who would come and go along with the Tidwells.

Funding was secured from various sources, some from different ADRA offices in such donor countries as Canada, European countries, the United States, and Australia.

There were food bank programs for the very elderly, the poor, and those in old peoples' homes. These facilities were very decrepit, old and run-down, and it was very sad to walk into these units. The men would be in one large room with maybe twenty or thirty beds, and the women were in a similar room. Health care was very minimal. So ADRA endeavored to provide assistance for these disenfranchised older people.

The same conditions prevailed in the orphanages. Quite a number of orphanages in and around Ho Chi Minh City needed help, and ADRA was able to provide various types of assistance to the orphans in these homes.

Over a period of time, projects were developed in some of the areas surrounding Ho Chi Minh City. Provinces that desperately needed health care and training were given considerable assistance through the auspices of ADRA. Clinics were built. They were actually more like mini-hospitals with four to eight beds. Babies would be delivered there, and minor surgeries performed, but these little rural clinics were the only source of health care for thousands of villagers who lived in the surrounding community.

ADRA also helped to supervise the training of health-care personnel with workshops, training sessions, and seminars to help upgrade the medical staff in these small clinics.

Shortly after the ADRA office was established in Ho Chi Minh City, we were able to bring groups of individuals into Vietnam to see firsthand the activities that were being carried out by ADRA/Vietnam. The purpose was two-fold: first, to give these individuals who represented various church organizations in North America an opportunity to see what ADRA was doing in developing countries. It is one thing to read about the work and ministry of ADRA, but it is another thing to get a close-up view of what the organization is actually doing in these various countries. These groups would visit a number of countries in Southeast Asia, including Vietnam. Secondly, after spending a few days visiting the projects, talking to people who had benefited from the ministry and services of ADRA, talking to ADRA staff, and meeting with government officials, invariably these individuals would leave believing that the ADRA staff was not only accomplishing a noble and truly compassionate work but warranted their support, both morally and financially. Sometimes these groups would be willing to take on a significant project, raise money for it, and thus provide the support that was needed to build a clinic or help develop some small industry or cooperative venture.

In 1992 the church administrators in the Southern Union Conference of Seventh-day Adventists, the region that covers primarily the southeastern portion of the United States from the Carolinas to the Gulf states and Florida, sent a delegation to visit family church-funded projects in the Far East, including projects that were being sponsored by ADRA. This delegation was headed by Malcolm Gordon, president of the Southern Union, executive secretary Ward Sumpter, and chief financial officer Richard Center. These men, along with the heads of such institutions as the Adventist Health systems, Adventist universities, and conference presidents, spent three weeks visiting some of the key countries in Southeast Asia.

Needless to say, this trip was really an eye-opener. For some it was their first trip to Asia. The contrast between the different countries they visited was the difference between night and day—from the beautiful, modern, hustling, bustling, sanitized city of Singapore to the poverty-ridden areas of Bangladesh. Unless an individual has been there to see and experience it, it's very difficult to describe. This was also true of Indochina—Vietnam, Cambodia, and Laos. These countries have been ravished by war and conflict for decades, and as a result, millions of people were living in the very poorest of conditions. They desperately needed help. This was the primary reason ADRA was working in these countries.

Humanitarian aid is not just assisting at the time of a crisis, such as a cyclone, a typhoon, or an earthquake. As critical and important as that is, it is even more important to assist in the development of these areas, including literacy training where needed, mother/child health, childhood survival, food security issues, microenterprise development—a whole wide range of training programs that assist in propelling people upward to self-support, self-sufficiency, and self-respect. This requires major commitments of financial support and adequate staffing.

After the Southern Union staff had spent a number of days in Ho Chi Minh City, they had a far better understanding of what was being done, not only in Vietnam but also across Southeast

Asia, as they returned to their homes and offices in the southern United States.

Shortly afterward, at a meeting of the Southern Union executive committee, these leaders gave a report of their trip to Southeast Asia, and the committee voted unanimously to adopt a sister relationship in which the Southern Union, representing the southeastern United States, would adopt the Southeast Asia Union in the Far East as a sister organization. This relationship would eventually include visits from key church and lay leaders and lead to fund-raising in the Southern Union territory for projects in Southeast Asia. From the time of that first visit until the present, well in excess of one million dollars has been raised by the union and conferences in the Southern Union for programs and projects in Southeast Asia. Can you imagine the blessing that has been, not only to the people of these countries but also to organizations such as ADRA and the Seventh-day Adventist churches in Asia?

Some of the local conferences likewise have adopted certain areas of Southeast Asia as their own special projects. One of these is the Gulf States Conference, which includes the churches in Alabama, Mississippi, and the panhandle of Florida. These states, through the leadership of conference president Mel Eisele, have generated thousands upon thousands of dollars for projects in Vietnam, projects that not only benefit the people in various communities through the auspices of ADRA but also directly assist some churches that were in critical need.

Some churches that had been damaged during the war were still not fully renovated and rebuilt. Some churches needed major reconstruction and additions. Medical and dental clinics, too, have been financed completely or partially by the support of leaders and church members in the Gulf States Conference. This has been a tremendous encouragement to the members and church leaders in Vietnam.

It's sometimes difficult to describe the conditions under which these dear people have to work. The government publicly states that the Vietnamese constitution allows full religious freedom, but in practice this is not the case. To this date the government has still not given full recognition to the Seventh-day Adventist Church in Vietnam. Along with some of our top denominational leaders, I have met with the government officials that provide oversight to religious organizations in the entire country. We have urged them to provide recognition, but to this date it has not been done. Communist governments in these countries are very reluctant to put an official blessing on religious organizations, and this is a problem not only for Seventh-day Adventists but for other Protestants and for Catholics as well.

It is virtually impossible to move pastors from one area to another in Vietnam today. Once a pastor has been assigned to a certain city, he is pretty well locked in until either retirement or death. It is difficult for church leaders and pastors to travel around the country. Even today, permission must be secured for an individual to leave his particular area. Government officials will still come and interrogate church leaders and pastors from time to time, particularly if visitors come into the country from abroad and contact them without the government being fully aware of their visit. "Why did they come here?" "What did they do?" "What did they see?" These are the kinds of questions our leaders have to deal with even today, in spite of the fact that the SRVN has diplomatic relations with most Western countries, including the United States.

So it is sometimes easy to overlook the fact that in a number of these countries it is difficult for our leaders and pastors to do their work. But in spite of this, the church in the SRVN is growing. Hundreds are joining the church and becoming Seventh-day Adventist Christians every year. Even though their income is very, very meager, many of these members are very faithful in supporting the church with their tithes and offerings. One wonders how they can do so when they have so little to live on. We have churches up in the mountains of Vietnam, tribal areas called the Montagnard. Many churches in this region have members who live very frugally, just from hand to mouth. They are poor yet generous in their support of the church and its ministries. They are grateful for the help they get from Mrs. Le Thi Bach and for Vacation Bible Schools that are conducted and for branch Sabbath Schools that are held, for the little companies that are springing up and the many little home churches. This is how the message of Jesus and His love and grace is being shared in these remote areas of Vietnam.

After a number of years of being headquartered in Ho Chi Minh City, the ADRA International staff and the government officials felt it was best to move the main office from Ho Chi Minh City to Hanoi, Hanoi being the capital of the SRVN. And so the transition was made; our staff, consisting of Dennis and Lila Tidwell and Kim Mai, moved bag and baggage, office equipment, and personal effects to Hanoi. An apartment complex was found, and an office established. The new location made it much more convenient for the ADRA staff to work with government officials inasmuch as the primary ministries that provide services for the entire country are located in Hanoi.

As visits were made by the ADRA staff and others to Vietnam, a stopover in Hanoi was now necessary as well as visits to other areas of the country, such as Ho Chi Minh City. The change that has taken place in Hanoi since my first visit in 1988 has been spectacular. Investors from all over Southeast Asia, as well as from the Western world, have plowed resources into Hanoi. Beautiful new hotels, high-rise office buildings, condos, and shopping plazas have sprung up in recent years. Parts of the city are still the same as they were fifty or sixty years ago, but there is a new ultramodern part of Hanoi that has attracted investors. And the reason is obvious. Vietnam is a large country with a population of about eighty million. It is extremely beautiful, with famous beaches along the east coast right up to Danang, the China Beach area, and cool refreshing mountains in a hot, humid, tropical part of the world.

The lush, fertile delta region in the south produces rice crops that are among the most bountiful and productive in Asia. The country's resources have unlimited potential for development. So investors are coming in. The tourist trade is big business these days as well. Former servicemen who were in Vietnam with the U.S. military from the early 1960s to the cease-fire are returning to visit. They come with their families, children, and even grandchildren to visit this land that was once a hostile environment for them.

The attitude of the Vietnamese people toward Westerners, particularly Americans, is extremely positive, interestingly enough. One doesn't sense the hostility, anger, or hatred one might expect from people of two countries that were in major conflict over a period of years. The younger generation, both Vietnamese and American, know nothing of the conflict of the 1960s and 1970s except what they read in history books or what their parents and grandparents have told them. The Vietnamese young people have no personal knowledge of the war. The ones who recall it all too well are the middle-aged and the elderly, and by and large they have put it behind them. So it's good to see the warmth and the friendship and the bonding that is taking place between the Vietnamese and Americans and other Westerners.

The Vietnamese are a wonderful people, outgoing and gregarious for the most part, optimistic, less inhibited, more inclined to reveal their emotions—cry when they're sad, laugh and smile when they're happy. This is in contrast with some of their neighbors in countries not too far away, where the people are much more stoic, reserved—less expressive and gentle.

The ADRA office in Hanoi still faces a tremendous challenge in securing adequate funding for needed projects. As the years go by, donor countries such as the United States, Australia, Canada, and the Scandinavian countries are less inclined to fund projects in a country such as Vietnam because they see the economy and living conditions there improving. This is to be expected. At the same time, there are areas of tremendous need and opportunity that still deserve financial support.

Meanwhile, changes occurred in the ADRA staff. The Tidwells left for another assignment with ADRA in India where Dennis and Lila had lived as children. Another couple—Roger and Pam Kopitzke—was assigned to head up the office in Vietnam. They served as the ADRA directors for Vietnam, residing in Hanoi and working closely with Kim Mai, the associate director. The staff grew, and other staff members were involved in leadership positions in the Hanoi office. During this time, the group from the Southern Union was privileged to visit different ADRA projects, not only in the southern part of Vietnam but in the Hanoi region as well. It's fascinating to see key government officials visit these projects and hear their words of appreciation and high regard for the ministry that ADRA is providing throughout the country.

The major areas of strength for the Seventh-day Adventist Church lie in the central and southern parts of Vietnam, from the highlands down to the delta. The reason, of course, is the demarcation that existed for so many years between North Vietnam and South Vietnam. The North was under the domination of Communism, while the more open and democratic South made it possible for the church to carry on its missionary and evangelistic endeavors. The medical work, along with a school of nursing, began in Saigon, or Ho Chi Minh City as it is now called. There was a publishing house with literature evangelists distributing material from the DMZ down to the southern tip of Vietnam. There were schools and an educational system from first grade through junior college level. College-aged students who could qualify found themselves in Southeast Asia Union College in Singapore or in schools in the Philippines or India. Today it is difficult for young people in Vietnam to receive a Christian education. Church-sponsored schools are not allowed. Church-related publishing houses do not exist. Religious organizations are not permitted to operate health-care facilities. So this type of outreach is difficult and virtually impossible for Christian organizations to carry out at this time in Vietnam.

Kim Mai's daughter was finally able to secure a permit to leave Vietnam to further her education. Through the sponsorship of several individuals in the United States, she was able to attend the church-operated college in Pune, India. From there, she went on to the Philippines to secure additional graduate studies. Today she is employed as a faculty member at the Southeast Asia Union College, now referred to as Mission College, in Thailand, approximately two hours northeast of Bangkok. She and her husband, who is the dean of men at the college, are providing valuable service to the school. She has turned out to be a lovely, beautiful young lady, of whom her mother and all of us are very proud.

During the ensuing years, various organizations and groups that have been responsible for building either clinics or schools have had the opportunity to come to Vietnam for groundbreaking or dedication ceremonies. To see the smiles and the joyful expressions on the faces of the people that have benefited from these projects is reward enough for the financial sacrifices that many have made, not only individually but organizationally as well.

ESCAPE FROM SAIGON

I had the privilege recently of hosting a group that visited Vietnam, beginning in Hanoi where we were able to see a number of projects in the area, such as a school for blind children, a little industry that has been developed for blind adults to make brooms, as well as clinics and other projects. One of the interesting highlights of our trip was the opportunity to stay at the Hanoi Hilton. The Hanoi Hilton, the hotel, is located just around the corner from "Hanoi Hilton" the prison. U.S. prisoners of war, including John McCain, referred to the place they were incarcerated during the war as the "Hanoi Hilton." Today the prison has become a museum, and guests are able to walk through it and see the exact room where John McCain was held a prisoner. It's also possible to visit the museum that has been established by the SRVN to display the ravages of the war and the effects that the bombers had as they bombed the city of Hanoi during the conflict.

After viewing these historical sites, you come away deeply moved and with a horror of the inhumanity of war. But even as I pen these lines, conflicts are taking place in a number of areas around the world—the Congo, the Middle East, Afghanistan, Iraq, etc. These conflicts, unfortunately, will never cease as long as men hunger for power and dominion, and such traits will inevitably continue in human hearts until all this is concluded by the coming of Jesus.

In this group that was visiting Vietnam were a number of individuals who had been involved in the evacuation of Saigon. We had gone back for a reunion, to visit the Third Field Hospital, Tan Son Nhut airport, the headquarters church, and the compound where many of us had resided—and where the new hospital was being built. Included in this group were Dr. and Mrs. Weisseman, Don Roth, Royce Thompson, Pastor Le Cong Giao, and me. Our spouses were with us, so it gave us an opportunity to relive with them the trauma of that last week of April 1975.

Epilogue: Thirty Years Later

On Sabbath afternoon we decided to go over to the Third Field Hospital and see if we could get into the facility. I had been there a time or two before, but only for a very brief visit. The government has now turned this facility into a war museum. We parked the vehicle, walked around the side road, and came in from the back entrance where the ambulances had gone back and forth all during the night of the evacuation. You can imagine the emotions that swept over us as we walked into the compound. The building had not changed much. We walked up and down the long corridors, reminisced about where the kitchen and dining room facilities were, where the surgery suites were located, where the little chapel had been, etc. And we went up to the administrative offices, where we had had many a meeting, endeavoring to finalize the details of the evacuation. We took pictures and talked, remembering sometimes with laughter and sometimes with the same sensation in the pit of our stomachs that we had felt more than thirty years before. What a week that was!

And now the years have passed by. A new generation of Vietnamese has come of age. The group of 410 that arrived at Loma Linda University in early May 1975 have now scattered to the four winds. Many are located in Florida, quite a few in the Northwest, and many in the Northern California area, but the largest number have remained in Southern California—around Loma Linda as well as the Los Angeles and San Diego areas. There are eight or ten Vietnamese Seventh-day Adventist churches now in North America with a combined membership of several thousand. These have all sprung up as a result of that small group of 410 persons that landed at Pendleton Airbase in early May 1975.

A number of the elderly have died. Those of us who were involved in the evacuation are now gray and retired, but the memories linger. They will be with us forever. The friendships that were forged through the circumstances of that situation will continue throughout eternity. The kindness, love, and generosity shown by the people in the community of Loma Linda, California, as well as in other areas of the United States, to this ragtag group of refugees will never be forgotten. The Vietnamese people will always hold in high esteem their American brothers and sisters and deeply appreciate their kindness, gentleness, and generosity. It is a beautiful thing to see this. This is the way it should be—the way it will be on an even wider scale when Jesus returns and claims His children from the four corners of the earth, from every nation, language group, and culture. Then we will all be one because we are all His children.

Above: A giant Galaxy C-5A military transport plane takes off from Saigon's Tan Son Nhut Airport with 305 people aboard, most of them Vietnamese orphans destined for new homes in the United States. Below: Remains of the aircraft after it crashed just short of the airport runway. Only 127 persons survived. Those who died were mostly orphans (photos by UPI/Bettmann Newsphotos).

7 April 1975

Mr. Harvey Rudisaile
Hospital Administrator
Seventh Day Adventist Hospital
Saigon, Vietnam

Dear Mr. Rudisaile:

I find it quite difficult to adequately
express my personal gratitude and that of
my people for the superb medical attention
given the surviving victims of the recent
air tragedy that deprived us of so many of
our friends and the children they were
trying to help.

But for the professionalism, devotion, and
determination of your staff, that tragedy
might well have been total in its consequence.

Please accept our undying thanks and our
continued good wishes for your continued help
to this community.

Gratefully,

H. D. SMITH
Major General, USA
Defense Attache

Letter of Major General H. D. Smith to Harvey Rudisaile, administrator of
Saigon Adventist Hospital, thanking him for the medical attention that the hospital provided to survivors of the doomed orphan flight.

Clockwise from top: Ralph Watts at the time of the Vietnam evacuation; Pastor Le Cong Giao and his wife Anh prepare to leave Vietnam; Saigon Adventist Hospital (photo by Richard Weismeyer, Loma Linda University).

Loading the ambulance at Saigon Adventist Hospital that will take Vietnamese nationals to Tan Son Nhut Airport for evacuation to the United States.

A group of evacuees arrive at the airport—the first step on a long journey to the United States.

Clockwise from top: The bowling alley at Tan Son Nhut Airport in Saigon, where all evacuees from Vietnam congregated; Drs. James Simpson and Bruce Branson with Pastor Pham Thanh; Romie Gainer prepares to leave Vietnam; the children wonder when they will leave Vietnam.

In Guam. Top: Tent city where refugees lived. Bottom: Pastor Don Roth and Dr. Stewart Shankel check on a group.

Happy to be in America! (Photos by Richard Weismeyer, Loma Linda University.)

Within a few months of arriving in the United States, most the Vietnamese refugees had found homes and employment. Above: Pastor Le Cong Giao, shown here with his wife, Anh, became the pastor of a Vietnamese church in Los Angeles (photo courtesy of Southern California Conference of SDA). Below: A number of Vietnamese found employment at Pacific Press. Shown here are Loc Nguyen, Huyen Nuguyen, Chuc Huynh, and Chi Huynh (photo by Duane Tank, Pacific Press).

Vietnamese refugees arrive at the Loma Linda University campus in California on May 2, 1975, having just arrived from Saigon and Guam.

The delegation representing the Adventist Development and Relief Agency (ADRA) during the 1988 visit to Vietnam. Left to right: N. O. Matthews, General Conference Office of Public Affairs; George Johnson, chairman, ADRA Board, Southeast Asia Union; Le Cong Giao, former president, Vietnam Mission; Maitland DiPinto, director, ADRA, Far Eastern Division; Ralph S. Watts, president, ADRA International.

Ralph S. Watts with Mr. Quan from the American desk of the Ministry of Foreign Affairs. During the 1988 visit to Vietnam, Mr. Quan was the group's guide. He helped process customs papers and took care of many other complicated details.

Ralph S. Watts visiting with Mr. Can, director of the Vietnamese Foreign Ministry, North American Division.

Ralph S. Watts and Mr. Nien, vice minister for Foreign Affairs.

Pastor Le Cong Giao, Dr. Xuan, Minister of Health, and Ralph S. Watts. Tragically, Dr. Xuan was killed in an airplane accident only a few weeks after this photo was taken.

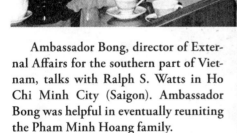

Ambassador Bong, director of External Affairs for the southern part of Vietnam, talks with Ralph S. Watts in Ho Chi Minh City (Saigon). Ambassador Bong was helpful in eventually reuniting the Pham Minh Hoang family.

Ralph S. Watts (center), and Pastor Le Cong Giao (right), with Madame Hao (left), the protocol officer for the Ministry of Foreign Affairs and the individual assigned to be their guide during their travels in the southern part of Vietnam in 1988.

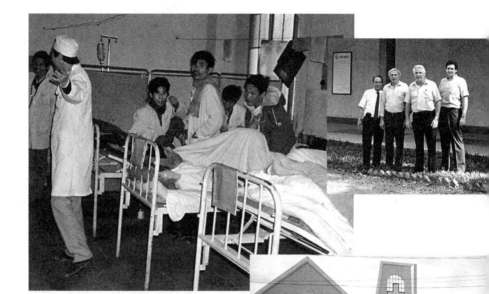

A typical Vietnamese hospital ward visited during the 1988 tour of medical facilities.

Members of the delegation stand in front of the hospital that the Adventist Church was building in Saigon at the time of the evacuation in 1975. The church never did occupy this facility. At the time of the cease-fire the church had been asked by the United States government to take over the operation of a large U.S. military hospital in Saigon.

The headquarters of the Seventh-day Adventist Church located in Saigon. This photo was taken in 1988.

Worshipers at the Saigon head-quarters Seventh-day Adventist Church. When the ADRA delegation met with these members in 1988 it was the first contact this group had had with any church leaders from outside Vietnam since the fall of Saigon in April 1975.

Ralph S. Watts, Pastor Le Cong Giao, and R. I. Gainer stand in front of the grave of Pastor Giao's father, Pastor Le Van Ut. Pastor Ut died a short time after his son left Vietnam for the United States in 1975.

Mrs. Pham Minh Hoang and er three children with Pastor iao. At the time of this photo-aph, this portion of the Hoang mily had been separated from astor Hoang and three other chil-ren for a number of years. The mily was eventually reunited.

The Hoang family some years after being reunited. Pastor and Mrs. Hoang (left), stand with Ralph S. Watts (center), and three of their six children and one grandchild.

Ralph S. Watts (far left), R. I. Gainer (kneeling center), and Pastor Giao (far right) bid farewell to Adventist leaders and members at the Tan Son Nhut airport at the conclusion of the 1988 visit.

Ralph S. Watts and the local Vietnamese provincial governor officiate at the opening of a medical clinic built under the auspices of the Adventist Development and Relief Agency (ADRA) in February 1999.

ADRA leadership meets with the Minister of Social Affairs for the Socialist Republic of Vietnam.

Kim Mai, associate director of ADRA/ Vietnam, dressed in the traditional Vietnamese *ao dai.*

Ralph S. Watts and Malcolm Gordon, president of the Southern Union of Seventh-day Adventists, cut the ribbon to open a clinic funded by the Southern Union in the United States.

Roger and Pam Kopitzke with Ralph S. Watts in Vietnam in the late 1990s. The Kopitzkes served as directors for ADRA/Vietnam, residing in Hanoi and working closely with Kim Mai, the associate director.

An emotional meeting between Johnny Johnson and Ralph S. Watts decades after the fall of Saigon in 1975. Johnny Johnson is the U. S. government official who worked with Pastor Watts to approve the 410 names of those Vietnamese individuals who eventually were cleared to leave Saigon in the evacuation of 1975.

Pastor Giao, Johnny Johnson, and Ralph S. Watts. Mr. Johnson is now retired and living in Alabama.

Johnny Johnson with Pastor and Mrs. Giao and two of their children.

In a recent visit to Vietnam, Pastor Giao stands with Ralph S. Watts in the church last pastored by his father, Pastor Le Van Ut. The church was heavily damaged during the war.

A recent picture of Pastor Giao and his wife, Kim, whom he married after the death of his first wife, Anh.

Pastor and Mrs. Ralph S. Watts with Kim Mai who now serves as assistant pastor of the San Jose, California Vietnamese Church. For many years Kim Mai provided outstanding leadership as associate director of ADRA/Vietnam.